**LAWRENCE L. STEINMETZ**
Graduate School of Business Administration
University of Colorado

# INTERVIEWING SKILLS FOR SUPERVISORY PERSONNEL

**ADDISON-WESLEY PUBLISHING COMPANY, INC.**
Reading, Massachusetts · Menlo Park, California
London · Amsterdam · Don Mills, Ontario · Sydney

ISBN 0-201-07280-7
EFGHIJKLMN-AL-798765

# Preface

Studies prove that the industrial supervisor today spends approximately 75% of his time communicating. A large percentage of that time is spent in formal and informal interviews—facts must be determined, an employee must be assigned a new task, a new man needs coaching, and so forth.

Because most supervisors have had little or no training in the skills required to interview effectively, this book has been written. It has as its purpose the development of simple, easy-to-learn techniques which the supervisor can apply to his job. No effort is made in this book to make a big production of the simple task of interviewing; no attempt is made to unduly belabor fine points of differences in style, purpose, or benefit of one kind of interview over another. Rather, the intent is to develop, in simple language, the down-to-earth techniques of successful interviewing—techniques which the supervisor can teach himself.

This book has been designed to elaborate on what interviewing really is in its basic forms and how these various forms can be utilized by the operating supervisor. The supervisor, the people he works with, and the company he works for can profit from his enhanced communication skills. If the reader of this book is interested in an even more comprehensive presentation of the subject of interviewing, complete with audio-visual aids, his attention is directed to Addison-Wesley Publishing Company's INTERVIEWING SKILLS Filmstrip Series. This book was written to be compatible with that series of six filmstrips, which Martin Broadwell has so very usefully developed. If the Filmstrip Series is used in conjunction with this book, the reader will find that he has a more thorough and exhaustive understanding of the skill of interviewing than he would get from any intensive management training seminar on the subject of interviewing.

Whether the reader uses this book singly or in conjunction with the Filmstrip Series, a special note must be added about the role-playing cases included at the end of the book. These cases represent real incidents in which supervisors have had to exercise interviewing skills. Each supervisor's role, therefore, can be used to benefit anyone interested in developing interviewing skills. Furthermore, the role-playing cases, if used properly, are virtually guaranteed learning experiences. There is no possible way—whether played poorly or well—that a person playing a role can avoid becoming interested in the action of the situation. As the role player discovers why he did well or poorly, he will learn. The experience will reinforce the techniques he handles well and enable him to avoid making mistakes on the job.

In doing the research to develop and write this book, it became obvious to me that much has been said about interviewing, but much that is said is confusing or unduly pedantic. It is my sincere wish that this book does not force the reader to suffer cutting through oblique verbiage in an effort to understand how to improve his skills as a supervisor. In accomplishing this aim, I wish to express my appreciation to the many people who have read and edited the manuscript, and/or advised me concerning the content of this book. Particular thanks go to the staff of Addison-Wesley Publishing Company, to the reviewers of the manuscript and, of course, to my wife and family for having the patience to assist me in seeing this work to fruition.

*Boulder, Colorado*                                                    L. L. S.
*May 1971*

# Contents

**PART VII    HOW TO RATE YOURSELF ON YOUR INTERVIEWING SKILLS**

**Practical Guide and Checklist**

**PART VIII    ROLE-PLAYING CASES FOR PRACTICE INTERVIEWS**

**Case 1    Conducting a Job Interview: The Owens Printing Company**

**Case 2    Employment Interview: Mary Jones, Secretary**

**Case 3    An Information-Gathering Interview: The Coffee Problem**

**Case 4    A Disciplinary Interview: The Water Boy**

# PART I    INTRODUCTION

# Chapter 1     Interviewing as a Specialized Skill

"Good management requires only the application of common sense," say the people not trained in practical management techniques. Many people believe that anyone with a little common sense can intuitively perform well any of the specific functions of management—including the job of interviewing.

To anyone experienced in practical management, however, it is obvious that doing a good job of managing takes more than just using common sense. In fact, those who have reached management levels have found that many tools and techniques of managing had to be learned before they were able to perform effectively. Interviewing is one of these tools and techniques that requires specialized skills.

## WHAT IS AN INTERVIEW?

An interview, broadly defined, is a two-way communication system. A business interview involves the giving and getting of information relevant to the conduct of work. Successful interviewing by a manager or supervisor can, therefore, be defined as the art of "making conversation with a purpose."

Basically, there are five different kinds of interviews with which a supervisor may find himself involved: (1) employment interviews, (2) counseling interviews, (3) disciplinary interviews, (4) performance appraisal interviews, and (5) exit interviews.

## EMPLOYMENT INTERVIEWS

The purpose of an employment interview is to get as much pertinent information as possible from the applicant. Employment interviews, therefore, are usually quite broad in scope because a great variety of information is being sought about an individual's background and personality. Information which the supervisor must get includes supplementary data about the work history of the applicant, his mental attitudes, his ability to relate to others, his family situation, and so forth. In other words, he must bring out any information not clearly stated on the application blank or disclosed by testing, and any not likely to be revealed in the reference check. The applicant himself may have questions about the work or management policies. Thus we have a situation where information is both sought and given by both interviewer and interviewee.

## COUNSELING SITUATIONS

Counseling interviews between a boss and a subordinate usually deal with the subordinate's job performance, attitudes, or behavior. While the scope of the counseling interview may be quite broad, it is usually reasonably narrow. Counseling interviews can be extremely broad when the cause of a problem with an employee is hard to identify. For example, if an employee is exhibiting a general feeling of disinterest in his work, the discussion may encompass a broad area. His disinterest in his work may spring from a variety of sources, ranging anywhere from dissatisfaction with his home life, worry about being automated out of a job, or concern with social unrest. In such a situation, the supervisor may touch on a variety of subjects in order to discover the underlying causes of the trouble and deal effectively with the employee.

Usually when a supervisor counsels with a subordinate, it is about a particular problem such as the man's inability to delegate work effectively to his subordinates, his reluctance to assume responsibilities on the job, or his personality conflict with a co-worker. In cases like these, the scope of the interview is narrow and can be confined to specific incidents and ideas.

The purpose of counseling is to correct less-than-satisfactory performance, alleviate fears, or otherwise handle specific job performance problems— whether they have to do with mechanical skills or personality problems. The objective is to find out what is causing an employee's performance to be less than satisfactory, to get him to recognize what his job difficulties happen to be, and to stimulate him toward improving marginal or unsatisfactory performance. The objective of the counseling interview, in short, is to alter behavior. The interviewer must assess the employee's suitability for performing a particular job, discover what his shortcomings are, what causes them, and how he can help the person to improve in those areas in which he is weak.

## DISCIPLINARY SITUATIONS

The disciplinary interview situation is quite different from that of the employment or counseling situation. The purpose of the disciplinary interview is to clarify a problem situation and initiate steps to correct it. The disciplinary interview is action-oriented; it is designed to effect immediate improved performance by an individual or group of individuals. Usually it is confined to a single person and to a particular disciplinary problem. Perhaps, for example, an employee has come in tardy three times during the week or has been guilty of fighting, horseplay, or drinking on the job.

The objective of the disciplinary interview is clearcut: changed behavior. The fact that the objective is clear-cut and the scope limited makes the situation appear routine to an observer. Someone gets angry, emotions run high, personal sensitivities are triggered, and the situation often becomes a "You'll listen—I'll talk" type of operation. High emotions and strained nerves are not necessary in disciplinary interviewing situations. Although the wise manager knows that such conditions often do exist, he realizes that there is a better way to handle them. More will be said about this later.

## PERFORMANCE APPRAISAL AND REVIEW

Performance appraisal interviews are conducted to review and evaluate a subordinate's performance. The scope of this kind of interview usually is quite broad. A man's performance and his potential with the company must be evaluated and discussed. The content of the interview may range anywhere; it may include a discussion of evening courses the person is taking or contemplates taking, his past and probable salary, the possibilities for job skill improvement, or the health of the employee's spouse, parents, or children.

For you as the supervisor, there are important advantages in appraising and reviewing a person's performance. You can keep a "scorecard" on how the man is performing his job. Even a set of notes or comments will provide a record for reference at some future time. You will have at hand information for assessing the man's potentialities on his current job or possibly for a different one in the future. This type of interview also gives you an opportunity to motivate the person toward better performance.

The objective of performance appraisal is clear—to let the guy know how he is doing. You should give the man an idea as to where he is in the organization, how he is doing, and where he is going. Unfortunately, having a definition of what the objective of the performance appraisal or review situation is doesn't necessarily mean you will accomplish this objective. Some supervisors behave as if they believe the purpose is to conduct either an uncomfortable ritual, required by higher management just to keep the supervisor "on his toes." Others use performance appraisal review as a legitimate excuse to unload their own feelings. They expect the subordinate to sit there and take it, and assume that he will react positively by displaying improved performance. This is not a very good approach, as we shall see.

## EXIT INTERVIEWS

Exit interviews are held with employees who have given notice to leave or who have been fired. They are designed to find out what the employee's true feelings are about the company, the working environment, and other job conditions. The information gathered may help prevent the future loss of valued employees, improve hiring policies, validate the criteria used in placing certain types of people in certain jobs, check the thoroughness of the company's training program, and get some assessment of the quality of supervision being given employees.

Two of the primary purposes of interviewing are to predict the behavior of someone or to control his behavior. However, no matter what the major purpose of the interview, all interviewing situations should have several similar characteristics. These include

1. Clearly defined purposes or objectives,

2. A plan as to how to attain the objectives sought, and

3. Good rapport between the interviewer and the interviewee.

## GENERAL RULES FOR EFFECTIVE INTERVIEWS

Considering the foregoing list of similarities in all good interview situations, we can list the following requirements for an effective interview:

1. The interviewer must be determined to *listen* to the other person. He must *not* do all the talking.

2. He must create a feeling of trust and confidence with the interviewee. Fairness and honesty must genuinely exist.

3. The interviewee must be put at ease. Some "small talk" usually helps to satisfy this requirement.

4. The reason for the interview must be clear in the minds of both the interviewer and the interviewee.

5. Words and phrases used must have a common meaning to both interviewer and interviewee.

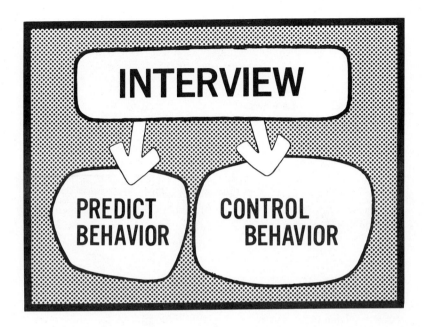

6. The room should be comfortable and well lighted, with no glaring lights or loud noises.

7. The interviewer should be able to sit facing the interviewee. Eye-to-eye contact is important.

8. The interviewer must give his undivided attention to the interviewee. He should not attempt to do other work while conducting the interview. As far as possible, there should be no interruptions, from the telephone or any other source.

If the above rules are carefully followed, it is unlikely that a person will conduct a poor interview, no matter what the purpose of the interview. However, it is important to recognize that interviews do differ as to their major purposes, and consequently are conducted differently. Let us examine some of these differences.

## BASIC KINDS OF INTERVIEWS

### Information-Gathering Interviews

Basically, supervisors are called upon to conduct three major kinds of interviews. One is the information-gathering type in which the major purpose is to get information from the other person.  The exit interview is a good example of the information-gathering interview because its purpose is to determine why an employee is leaving and what his feelings are toward the company.

## Information-Giving Interviews

The second kind of interview is that which is meant to give information to the interviewee.  The classic example is the indoctrination interview given when a new employee is hired or immediately afterward.  Information is given to the person about starting time, quitting time, coffee-break time, how and when he will be paid, when he will be covered under company insurance programs, and information about the requirements of his job.  The intent, of course, is to impress upon the employee particular information which he will need in doing his work.

## Problem-Solving Encounters

A third kind of interview that a supervisor must often conduct is the problem-solving type.  The purpose of this kind of interview is both to get and to give information in an effort to solve a problem.  An example of the problem-solving interview occurs when a supervisor must investigate and make a decision about a disciplinary problem.  If there are opposing points of view as to what happened, the interviewer must get information from all parties concerned, try to determine the truth about what did happen, and then give information as to his decision about the matter.

## TECHNIQUES OF INTERVIEWING

Primarily, three different techniques are used in interviewing.  Quite naturally, any specific supervisor will prefer one more than another because of his basic approach to people, his prior training and exposure to interviewing processes, and his fundamental view of human nature.  Each of the three techniques, however, is useful and has a great deal of merit when applied in the proper situation.  These three techniques of interviewing are: (1) the directed interview, (2) the nondirected interview, and (3) the stress interview.

## The Directed Interview

One technique used by supervisors we call the directed interview.  For this procedure the interviewer must have not only a preconceived notion of

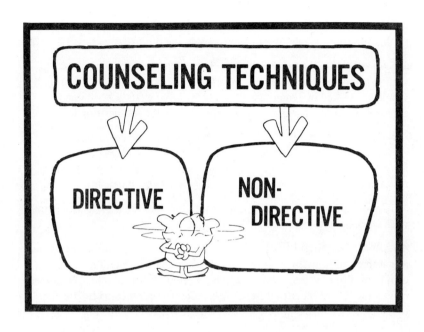

what he wants to accomplish, but what steps he plans to follow. He may
even have a topical outline of the subjects he wishes to talk about. He
sets about the discussion in a methodical way and follows a fairly rigid
procedure whether his purpose is to get information, to give information,
or to solve a problem.

Many times the directed interview is not well received by the interviewee.
One of the shortcomings comes about because of the abruptness or the
impersonal approach of the interviewer. The supervisor who depends on
the directed interview may be stilted in approach or unduly authoritative.
Unfortunately, many supervisors are more comfortable in a directed interview situation; with this technique they have something to lean on and
a feeling of being in control of the situation. The directed interview does
have the advantage of thoroughness, however, and thus is an essential
interviewing technique.

**Example of a directed interview.**   As can be seen in the following dialogue,
the interviewer uses frank, matter-of-fact questions. This is a thorough
and concise method of gathering information. In the following case, a
young man is being interviewed for a job as a clerk in a ski shop. The

reader should observe that the interviewer controls the discussion entirely; he does not permit the interviewee to guide the discussion.

*Mr. Jones* (manager of the ski shop): Let's begin by reviewing some of your previous work experience, Art. I see on your application form that you have worked in a men's clothing store. What exactly were you responsible for and what ordinary, routine duties did you perform?

*Art Morrison:* Primarily I was a sales clerk, waiting on customers. However, I also helped with stocking the store, taking inventory, and so forth. My major responsibilities were greeting customers, helping them find the merchandise they wanted, and then writing out sales slips.

*Mr. Jones:* What do you really think that you were the best at while you were working with customers?

*Art:* Well, the things I felt I did best were in areas where you had to sell a customer on something, or at least help him make a decision between a couple of different items which he had in mind. For example, a customer may come in and think that he wants a suit. The problem is getting him to really decide on a suit and actually buy it—transfer him from "looker" to "buyer." I feel that my main strength was in the area of actually closing the sale with customers.

*Mr. Jones:* That sounds good, Art. Tell me a little something about what you don't like doing, or at least didn't like doing in selling clothing.

*Art:* I suppose the thing that I liked least of all was having to repackage merchandise or straighten it out after somebody had fumbled through it. That kind of got on my nerves, especially when I would see people with dirty hands start rummaging through new stuff. Invariably they would soil something which ultimately we couldn't sell or certainly would have to mark down. I'd say that I enjoyed that the least.

*Mr. Jones:* Well Art, let's change the subject here a little bit and talk about something else. I would like to know something about the relationships you have with other people. For example, how about the boss that you had in the clothing store? What did you think were his strengths and weaknesses?

*Art:* Well, I would say that his strong point was that he was very easy to get along with. He never got up tight about things that would go wrong. For example, like when you would make a mistake writing up a sales slip or something. He was always kind in helping you recognize what your mistakes were and trying to correct them.

*Mr. Jones:* I see, Art. Tell me a little something about his major weaknesses.

*Art:* Well, I couldn't really say that he had any major weaknesses, and I would hate to be forced into criticizing Mr. Krenzel. After all he was a pretty congenial fellow, and he always understood when you had some kind of problem and perhaps needed some time off or couldn't come in to work right on time or something.

*Mr. Jones:* I see. Tell me about the kinds of people that you like to work with. For example, describe an individual that you really think would be a good fellow employee.

*Art:* Oh, I don't know. A guy who is kind of "in" on things. He shouldn't take life too awfully seriously, but I think that a guy should have a little ambition. I think he should enjoy working and be the kind of guy who would help out someone else on occasion.

*Mr. Jones:* Art, tell me a little about your family and personal interests. I see that you are not married. Do you have plans for getting married? Also, are you living alone or is this address also your parents' address? It's not clear to me on the application blank.

*Art:* Yes, I'm on my own, or at least not with my parents, if that's what you mean. I have an apartment with a couple of other fellows. In respect to the question of getting married, no, I don't have any present plans for doing so. However, I do date a girl rather regularly.

*Mr. Jones:* I see. What do you do for recreation?

*Art:* Well, in the wintertime I like to ski, naturally. Why else would I be looking for a job in a ski retail store? However, in the summertime I like to camp and hunt, and I also like water skiing just to stay in shape. During the wintertime if I don't get enough skiing in, I like to play basketball.

**Comment on the sample directed interview.** The general drift of the sample dialogue illustrates the directed interview. It should be clear to the reader that Mr. Jones directs the interview by following a rather rigid outline as to the information that he wants to get, and that he completely controls the interview. Such an interview technique is good in most cases when it is especially desirable to gather information which might not otherwise be volunteered.

You should note, however, that the interviewer did not pursue certain items which he probably should have. One item of interest would be the comment Art made concerning the fact that his prior supervisor was a pretty good fellow to work for because he was understanding when Art needed time off. This information should have been followed up by Mr. Jones because it could indicate that Art may expect to be given time off work on occasion—or at least may not be 100% reliable when it comes to getting to work on time, regularly, every day. Mr. Jones could have pursued that point during the interview by leaving his structured outline temporarily, or he might have made a note to come back to it later. In either event, the subject should be pursued before a final decision is made to hire Art.

Another interesting response was the suggestion by Art that the reason he wants to work in a ski shop is because he likes to ski. It is an established fact that one should be interested in the work that he does, and Art's interest in skiing might be important. However, to the extent that most ski retailers believe that one doesn't need to be a good skier to sell skis, there is reason to believe that this attitude of Art's might be a negative rather than a positive feature. He may be wanting to get a job in a ski shop simply to get a good discount on merchandise for himself, rather than because he is seriously interested in full-time, long-run employment. This point should also have been pursued by Mr. Jones in determining Art Morrison's suitability for employment in the retail ski store.

## The Nondirected Interview

An extreme example of a nondirective type of interview might be the stereotype of the bartender listening to a customer. He is sympathetic and understanding, nonauthoritarian, and attentive; he listens and rarely offers advice. All these characteristics may be found in the nondirective interview. Here the interviewer gives the other person a good deal of leeway in expressing his thoughts. The idea behind the nondirective technique is that fundamentally (1) a person wants to talk about what he has on his mind, and (2) ultimately tells what he has on his mind if he is allowed to do so.

The nondirective interview technique must not be absolutely unstructured, however. While it may be true that a trained psychiatrist can let a patient ramble on and get meaning from the discussion, it is not true that the typical supervisor can get satisfactory results by just letting a subordinate talk. To begin with, time is too important to waste on nonessentials. The fact is that most supervisors who profit from nondirective techniques do have

in mind a general idea of what they want to find out. They usually guide the interview to some degree, certainly to the point of bringing the discussion back to the subject when the conversation wanders too far toward irrelevant topics.

It is important to recognize that even in the nondirective interview, a supervisor must have a clear-cut purpose in mind and know what he wants to accomplish from the interview. He simply does not follow an established structure or outline in accomplishing this objective. Conversation is permitted to run freely, but the major, relevant points are developed by the interviewer.

The obvious disadvantage of the nondirective interview is that the supervisor may forget to get or to give certain critical information unless he is highly skilled and very attentive. The big advantage of the nondirective interview is that it is conducive to an informal atmosphere and a general feeling of good-fellowship.

**Example of a nondirective interview.** The following is an example of a nondirective interview situation in an electrical contracting shop. The foreman is talking to an electrician who has just given his notice. The foreman is conducting an exit interview of the nondirective variety in order to find out why Bill Jones has just quit and why two other electricians have quit during the past two weeks.

*Foreman* (Al):  Bill, I appreciate your being willing to discuss with me why you are leaving.  You know I don't want you to go.

*Bill:*  Well, I'm a little reluctant to leave, but I just think that it's the thing to do.

*Al:*  Why do you think it's the thing to do?

*Bill:*  Well things haven't been going too well around here as you know . . .

*Al:*  In what way?

*Bill:*  Well, I don't know Al.  I just haven't been very happy since Gus and Dick left.

*Al:*  I can understand that you may not have been happy since Gus and Dick left, Bill, because I know that you were pretty close to them.  But would you fill me in on one thing—why do you think they left?

*Bill:*  Well, I really don't know why Dick left other than the fact that Gus got mad and quit.  But then you know that Dick and Gus were really close to each other.  I guess that it is just that we are getting a little too much pressure from Frank [the office expediter].

*Al:*  You say Gus quit because he was mad?

*Bill:*  Sure, Al.  He was damn mad.  Don't you know about the time Frank accused Gus of joy-riding in the pickup when he came back to the shop for another box when old man Bellows, over at Bellows' restaurant remodeling job, put in that change order to have an extra 220 outlet under his counter?

*Al:*  You say Gus was joy-riding . . . .

*Bill:*  No, he wasn't joy-riding.  He had to come back to get the box.  Frank said he was.

*Al:*  Well, what did Frank say?

*Bill:*  Well, the story that I got from Gus was that when Gus came into the shop to get the box, Frank just jumped all over him and really dressed him down.

*Al:*  You say that Frank really dressed Gus down?

*Bill:* Yeah. He called him a dummy and said that he was lazy and wasn't a fit electrician, anyway. Hell, we don't have to put up with that kind of stuff. We've got our union cards. You know as well as I do that there is not a better electrician in this town than Gus.

*Al:* You feel that you, Gus, and Dick are among the best electricians in town?

*Bill:* You darn betcha we are. We get good job offers every week or so from other contractors, and that's why Gus and Dick left and that's why I'm leaving.

*Al:* You really mean you are quitting because you are getting more money—meaning someone is paying higher than union scale?

*Bill:* Of course some people pay higher than union scale. How else do you expect to get these jobs done when you're working on a government contract and you have a deadline to meet and you will lose your retention fee if you don't get it finished on time?

*Al:* Well, then you would say that the real reason that Gus left is not because Frank chewed him out, but because he could get more money somewhere else. Is that correct?

*Bill:* I suppose that would be about right.

**Comment on the sample nondirected interview.**  As can be seen from the above nondirective interview, the foreman discovered a lot of information which he previously did not know. He did this by asking questions which were triggered by what the electrician had to say. For one thing, he found out that the men didn't especially like Frank. More importantly, however, he found out that some other employers were paying higher wages—in fact, wages above union scale—in an effort to pirate employees.

It should be obvious to the reader that the information which came out in this exit interview would be of immense value to the owner of the electrical shop. It gives him some information concerning Frank, but, more importantly, it tells him that if he is going to keep his good employees, he will either have to pay higher than union scale or do something to keep them loyal to the organization.

### Stress Interviews

A third technique, one used less frequently, is the stress interview. The stress interview relies on a series of tough, unexpected, anxiety-producing questions. These are designed to place the interviewee in a highly uncomfortable situation and force him to react instinctively. In the hands of a skillful interviewer, the other person will reveal his true personality and feelings.

The stress interview is most frequently used in pre-employment meetings, although it is sometimes used in counseling and disciplinary situations. The purpose of this technique is to find out how a man behaves under pressure. The theory is that if you put him in an extremely stressful situation, he will display his true colors. On the basis of the man's reactions, the interviewer can make some judgment about his temperament. For example, the interviewer may ask a pointed, biased question such as "Tell me the truth, they really fired you for stealing, didn't they?" How the man handles a question like this will show whether he is quick to anger, whether he is unduly submissive, whether he is a glib, fast talker, or whether he is a dullard who can't think on his feet.

It should be apparent that the stress interview would not be used very often, although it is useful in sizing up the personality and stability of a person. This technique is most commonly used in recruiting and selecting people for the upper levels of management.

**Demonstration of a stress interview.** The following is an example of a stress interview in which the supervisor is trying to get a reading on the emotional stability of a job applicant.

*Question* (by interviewer): Assume that tomorrow either you or your child must die. However, you have a choice as to which of you will die. Whom will you pick?

*Answer:* Well, I guess I would pick myself.

*Question:* Why?

*Answer:* Well, I don't know, it just seems like the thing to do. After all, I am older and have led a rather full life and, furthermore, I am reasonably well insured and my son would be fairly well taken care of financially.

*Question:* You mean you were the dupe of an insurance salesman who sold you something that you didn't need?

*Answer:* No! I bought the kind of insurance I need. After all, my insurance salesman is my brother-in-law, and he took careful pains to design a well-planned program for me.

*Question:* How can you justify buying insurance on the basis of nepotism?

*Answer:* I didn't buy it on the basis of nepotism! I bought what I needed from my brother-in-law.

*Question:* Isn't buying from your brother-in-law nepotism?

*Answer:* Not necessarily. It simply meant that I bought from someone that I could trust.

*Question:* You mean that most insurance salesmen are untrustworthy?

*Answer:* No. Simply that they don't always have your best interests at heart in selling you an insurance program.

*Question:* If someone doesn't have your best interests at heart, isn't he untrustworthy?

*Answer:* Not necessarily. I just don't understand what you mean.

*Question:* I don't think you know what you mean. Would you explain yourself a little better? After all, you said that you were over-insured, that your brother-in-law was your insurance salesman, that you thought he was trustworthy but that, after all, he is an insurance salesman, and that most insurance salesmen don't have the best interests of the buyer at heart.

*Answer:* I think, sir, that you have me all wrong. The original question was who would I elect to have die tomorrow, myself or my child. The answer is myself. The reason is not because I am over-insured, nor is it because I bought insurance from my brother-in-law, who may or may not be untrustworthy. The reason is because I feel that I have led a full and fruitful life and would be willing, in a forced choice situation, to elect to die so that my son might live, because he has not yet had the opportunity to live a full life.

**Comment on the sample stress interview.** As illustrated in the above script, the purpose of the stress interview is to put an individual in a stress-ful situation and force him to come up with answers to explain himself. The way he reacts to accusations, insinuations, and false assertions helps the interviewer determine the emotional stability of the individual. In the sample situation described, the interviewee took a badgering for a while, but ended very strongly by summarizing every point of the discussion. He did not yield to the badgering of the interviewer nor did he lose his temper. Assuming that the man was an applicant for a position requiring a force-ful, logical, and strong personality, he would receive a high rating as a result of the interview. Of course, if the purpose of the interview was to determine whether the individual was a compliant and nonassertive type, he would receive a low rating because of his emphatic comments and tendency to take control of the interview, as represented by the final remarks which he made.

**PART II**    ESTABLISHING RAPPORT AND
COMMUNICATING EFFECTIVELY

Of all the material published on interviewing, probably most emphasis is placed on establishing the interview relationship itself. Most authorities say that to be an effective interviewer one must establish good rapport with the interviewee. While this is very important, overdoing it in terms of the physical setting, excessive small talk at the beginning, and so forth, can do as much harm as good. Let us look at some basic procedures.

## ESTABLISHING RAPPORT WITH THE INTERVIEWEE

Whenever it is necessary to interview an employee or prospective employee, greeting the applicant in a warm and sincere manner is the first step. Most people going into an interview situation experience some uneasiness at the prospect—be it a job applicant who is tense and worried he won't get a job, or an employee who knows that he is in for a disciplinary session and is upset. If the interviewer seems cold or unapproachable at this point, problems will be compounded. If, however, the interviewee is greeted in a warm and friendly manner, is given a comfortable seat, and is extended the usual social courtesies, a good interview climate is created.

Unfortunately, in attempting to establish rapport with the interviewee, many supervisors make the mistake of depending too much on a routine kind of small talk. A common topic many managers use for making small talk with a prospective job applicant is the latest sports event. Although such a topic may be an excellent entree for someone who follows sports, it may not be even of interest to someone who knows little about sports. The topic may, in fact, make the applicant feel uneasy. In short, small talk is effective *only* when the subject is of interest to *both* the interviewee and the interviewer. Otherwise it may prove to be an obstacle in establishing rapport.

Using small talk to establish rapport is easier for a supervisor who is interviewing a subordinate of long standing. In this case, the boss should know what is of interest to his subordinate, whether sports, hobbies, or whatever. He can elect topics to which he knows the subordinate will respond. With a new job applicant, a good source for small talk subjects may be found on an application form if the candidate has completed one. By quickly looking the form over, the interviewer may discover that the interviewee indicated that his hobbies are playing chess and restoring antique automobiles. If clues like this are available, the interviewer can provide himself with sufficient topical matter to put the applicant at ease.

Some supervisors attempt to establish rapport with subordinates by using a pat, prepared set of introductory remarks or questions. While it is a good idea to have something in mind with which to break the ice, using a canned speech or a set of loaded questions is a waste of time. Introductory remarks in the interview situation really serve only two purposes: (1) to establish an atmosphere in which the interviewee knows he or she will at least be treated courteously and (2) to overcome possible defensive attitudes which the interviewee might bring to the meeting. Once it is clear to the interviewee that he is not to be flogged and that he will have an opportunity to express himself, the introductory remarks designed merely to establish rapport can be stopped and progress made directly into the heart of the interview. In short, it is important in establishing rapport with the interviewee only to develop a climate which will facilitate the transfer of information.

## GUIDELINES FOR ESTABLISHING EFFECTIVE RAPPORT

Some attention, therefore, must be devoted to establishing a decent level of rapport. The following guidelines can be used by the supervisor who is unfamiliar with establishing a good interviewing situation:

1. Greet the interviewee in a friendly manner.

2. Indicate by some definite sign or gesture where the person is to sit. See that he is as comfortable as possible. Glaring lights, reflections from pools of water, or uncomfortable chairs detract from a relaxed interview.

3. Make the main purpose of the interview clear, and assure the employee that he will be given an opportunity to be heard.

4. Try to talk to the interviewee at his level in terms he can understand. Don't try to impress him with your vocabulary.

5. Sit directly facing the interviewee. Neither of you should have to twist around to see the other. Eye contact is important.

6. Insofar as possible, the place selected for the interview should be away from noise and the observation of other people.

7. Avoid needless interruptions—especially from the telephone. Nothing is more irritating than having someone interrupt, especially when the outcome of the interview is critical in the eyes of the interviewee. His job may depend on it.

8. Be courteous. Don't attempt to do other work while the interview is being conducted. (Have you ever attempted to have a serious discussion with someone who is trying to read his mail at the same time?)

9. Have a firm idea of what the objectives of the interview are, and don't be afraid of using a guideline, check list, or other reminder de-

signed to ensure that a complete job will be done in getting and giving information.

## INSTILLING CONFIDENCE IN
## THE PERSON BEING INTERVIEWED

The effective supervisor will instill confidence in the employee that the interview will be fruitful and productive for *him* as well as for the interviewer. Instilling confidence in the employee depends on the extent to which both the interviewer and the interviewee share a feeling that they are working together on a common problem, even if they disagree on some basic points. If the interviewer is reasonably adept at instilling confidence, he can get across the feeling that he intends to help the other person or work with him even though extreme differences of opinions exist.

To establish effective communication, the supervisor must demonstrate a willingness to talk face-to-face with openness. He must have a general understanding of himself and the impact he has on others. He must have the capacity to empathize with others. In other words, he must try to put himself in the other person's shoes and understand things from the other person's point of view.

Another way the supervisor can instill confidence in an interviewee is by conveying an image of objectivity. He must also realize that the interviewee needs to express his feelings. The supervisor must be able to understand not just the words, but what the interviewee is really saying. Finally, to establish a good interview relationship, the supervisor must often use techniques designed to get a reluctant talker to talk. The following chapter will discuss techniques that will help the interviewer accomplish these purposes.

## Chapter 4

How to Improve Your Ability to
Communicate in the Interview

It is frequently stated that many difficulties are brought about because
people don't communicate well. One of the "sage" observations the young
and naive make is that "if people would only communicate better, there
wouldn't be wars, marital difficulties, and so forth." We are all aware of
the difficulties that occur as the result of poor communication. Unfortunately, even though we recognize the problem, very few people do anything about it, and even those who try have difficulty in interview situations. It is imperative that the supervisor understand the fine art of verbal
communication and know how to apply it in his job of handling people.

### WHAT IS VOCAL COMMUNICATION?

Vocal communication is the verbal exchange of ideas, feelings, and opinions between two or more people. It involves all the senses, not just hearing. It is the overall result not merely of words, but of facial expressions
and gestures; not just the words that are spoken, but the tone of voice in
which they are said. Vocal communication is a function of the whole
physical and environmental setting in which communication takes place.

An example of the importance of the physical setting on the effectiveness
of communication, over and above the words said, can be observed by
anyone who wishes to make a simple test. Observe, if you will, the behavior of an animal—say a dog—toward a person who doesn't like dogs but
who is, for the sake of his host, "tolerating" the pet and offering it a tid-
bit of food. Even though the dog-hater is saying "come here, pretty
pooch" the animal *knows* from observing the *behavior* of the dog-hater,

that the person really doesn't like him and is engaging in a sham. The pet may even reject the food. Such behavior, of course, is not instinctual, because obviously the dog would like the morsel of food. Rather, it is a result of the face-to-face relationship which the dog-hater has established with the animal. Even though the dog-hater is saying encouraging words, the animal sees through this and behaves accordingly.

The converse situation can also exist. Many times a proud hunter uses vulgar expletives in speaking to his dog when the animal has done a particularly fine job in the field, such as having found a downed bird in extremely high grass. The animal knows he is being rewarded by his master because of the friendliness of the master's voice, and the gestures he uses, *even though the words are vile.*

Communicating vocally with a person is not so much a function of one's vocabulary as it is of being able to make oneself understood and of understanding others. Thus, two major problems must be recognized before one can communicate effectively: (1) understanding one's own impact upon others and (2) being able to empathize or understand the other person's feelings. Let us look at each of these in turn.

### Understanding One's Own Impact on Others

It is essential in any interview situation that the supervisor have some understanding of the impact he has upon others. Most research in psychology discloses that very few people are really aware of the impact that they have upon other people. In fact, the general lack of understanding by managers of how they affect others has caused many corporations to send their managerial and supervisory personnel to courses on sensitivity training. The idea behind sensitivity training is to sensitize people to their impact on others.

The nature of a person's inability to understand accurately the impact he has upon other people can perhaps best be clarified here by an example. Everyone knows who the gossips are in any organization. They invariably go around telling all they know to anybody who will listen. Think now, if you will, about any gossips you know who perceive of themselves as being gossips! If you are honest in your assessment, you will realize that none of these gossips perceive themselves as being gossips.

Now, if you will, imagine the gossip's position when he is talking with his co-workers. If they perceive him as a gossip, what will his co-workers tell him? Will they tell him their innermost secrets? Will they even be honest about themselves? Would they let him know that they were thinking about quitting their job? It is not likely, because they know he will blab it around. The gossip's co-workers will be guarded about the information they give to such a person.

Now, imagine the situation where the supervisor is perceived as a ruthless company man. What will a subordinate who is planning to quit the company tell him if the boss asks what his plans are toward the organization? Obviously, the subordinate will not say that he is contemplating quitting. He may even deny the fact; he may lie through his hat, fabricate stories, and say that he intends to retire from the company forty years hence.

Your perception of yourself and the other person's perception of you will have a tremendous impact on your capability to communicate effectively in an interview situation. The boss who doesn't see himself as he really is or who erroneously sees himself as one of the boys, who thinks no one understands the fact that he is trying to manipulate people, who is unduly concerned about his relationship with his superior but not at all concerned about the subordinate he is interviewing, and so forth, will find that these attitudes of his, which he thinks are hidden from the subordinate, will, in fact, hamper him in conducting an effective interview.

In short, it is important to remember that even before you start an interview with a subordinate or a job applicant, the other person will have made a number of assumptions based entirely upon his perception of you. You will be working at a serious disadvantage unless you make some effort to perceive accurately the impact that you have as an individual and as a person in a managerial position.

## Empathizing with Others

The word empathy means to feel *with* the other person, not for him. Unfortunately, many managers confuse empathy with sympathy. Empathy does not mean feeling sorry for an individual. There is a great deal of difference between empathy and sympathy. The idea behind empathy is to endeavor to see things in the same light as the other person does. It is extremely important, therefore, that the supervisor know and understand how others feel and react to him and to specific situations.

A supervisor or manager must assume that the person being interviewed will attempt to defend his position and that he will have a preconceived set of attitudes and assumptions about the interviewer. He will perceive the interviewer as his superior in the specific job situation, or at least as a person with power over him; he may not know what the boss wants to discuss, and he may have certain fears about his future with the company and the impression he is making.

In addition to these uncertainties, other complications may occur. There may be language barriers, personality differences, general anxiety, biases, prejudices, and personality characteristics such as ambition and impatience. It is obviously extremely difficult for a supervisor to empathize quickly and easily with a subordinate. It is essential that the interviewer at least be aware of the various problems which can crop up.

## HOW TO EMPATHIZE MORE EFFECTIVELY

What advice can we give the interviewer who is attempting to empathize with the interviewee? A list of guidelines should certainly include, but not be limited to, the following:

1. Have in mind a good opening for the interview. You should obtain as much information as possible about the interviewee and the special issue at hand. All this information will help you determine the easiest way to get into the subject of the interview.

2. Be careful not to overtalk the client or lecture to him. One-sided discussions practically always prevent the interviewer from learning anything about the interviewee.

3. Cultivate the ability to listen attentively. Unless you listen effectively you will not be able to empathize with the other person.

4. Avoid drilling or cross-examining the interviewee. While it may be desirable to place the interviewee in a stressful situation to get a reading on his personality, it is impossible to empathize with an interviewee if one assumes the role of a Gestapo agent.

5. Give the interviewee an opportunity to sound you out. Recognize that he is entitled to understand how you feel. He may need to get a reading or assessment as to what your stance or position is, especially on a controversial subject, if he is to feel he is going to have a fair hearing from you.

6. Avoid making snap judgments about the interviewee's situation, attitude, or interpretation of the subject. Recognize that many

times people don't express themselves well vocally, and you may
make a mistake as to the qualities of the individual if you jump to
a conclusion.

7. Be nonjudgmental in your attitude toward the interviewee. You must
   try to indicate *neither* tacit approval nor categorical rejection of what
   an interviewee is saying if you want to understand the interviewee.

8. Recognize that the interviewee may be leaving as much unsaid as he
   is saying. Sometimes people lapse into periods of silence or otherwise
   fail to communicate effectively. Usually there is a reason for this.
   Possibly the person is just not a talkative individual. Silence may, however, indicate fear or anxiety, or at least uncertainty, as to whether or
   not he is appropriately answering your questions.

9. Reflect upon what the interviewee has said. It is a good idea to attempt to rephrase to the interviewee what he has said in an effort to
   make sure that you are understanding his true feelings. Catch phrases
   like "You feel that . . ." or "If I understand you correctly, you're
   saying . . ." are good ways to ensure that he is saying what he means
   and that you are understanding it correctly. You may find that what
   he thought he was saying and the message you have received are very
   different.

10. Give the interviewee an opportunity to formulate his own plan or ideas (or whatever) and express them to you in any case in which some plan of action is to follow. Having him do this will force him to summarize what you have been discussing and think constructively about the job itself and/or any problem that has come up.

Using these ideas should help to facilitate communication. If the supervisor can empathize well with the interviewee and if he has a reasonably good understanding of the impact he has upon others, he will become increasingly skillful as an interviewer. Effective communication is not all that is required for success in interviewing, however. Let us turn now to some of the other factors.

# Chapter 5     Communication: The Finer Points

One of the additional skills required for an effective interview relationship is the ability to convey an aura of objectivity. Unfortunately, many people consider themselves extremely objective when in fact they are not.

## CONVEYING AN IMAGE OF OBJECTIVITY

It is difficult to be objective in an interview because few of us are free from bias and emotion. Complicating matters is the fact that many people consider themselves emotionally unbiased and are blind to their own limitations. Josh Billings put this phenomenon in clear perspective when he said, "Every man has a perfect right to his own opinion, so long as it agrees with ours."

All of us are subject to various biases about mannerisms, dress, speech, race, and so forth. The problem, however, is not so much that you are unaware of having biases, as it is of not knowing the impact biases have in your reaction to people.

Biases and prejudice are particularly important in forming impressions, and these can be critical in an interview where you are meeting a person for the first time. Bias can work for or against the other person. If an interviewer is biased in favor of someone, that person benefits from the "halo" effect, that is, he will be evaluated higher than he should be. By contrast, if the interviewer is biased against someone, that person will suffer from the "horns" effect and be rated lower than he should be. This bias works both ways, of course, and affects the way the interviewee perceives and responds to the interviewer.

The supervisor must work diligently toward conveying an image of objectivity toward any interviewee. This does not mean that the interviewer should say things like "It is all right that you have long hair; I understand," or "I won't hold it against you that you are ten minutes late for our appointment." Such statements will more likely rattle the interviewee than not. The interviewer should, however, mentally check himself against what he knows are sources of minor irritation to him and attempt not to hold these things against the interviewee if it is at all possible.

## ALLOWING THE INTERVIEWEE TO VENTILATE HIS FEELINGS

Another of the finer points required in an effective interview relationship can be achieved by giving the interviewee an opportunity to ventilate his feelings. He should know that he will have the opportunity to express himself, to raise questions, or to say things which he feels should be included in the interview.

Some interviewers wait until the end of an interview to ask the interviewee if he has anything to say. They feel this gives the interviewee the opportunity to say all he feels the need to say. Unfortunately, this tactic does not work to best advantage in most situations. While it does serve to leave the door open for the man to speak his piece, usually the opportunity comes too late. The interview is nearly over, and the interviewee is apt to feel that nothing he says at that point will change the results of the interview. If the opportunity to express their feelings is given only at the end of the interview, many people go away feeling that they were not treated fairly. Thus, throughout the conduct of the interview you should ask the employee questions and give him an opportunity to talk whenever he indicates that he has something to say. The interviewer must be very sensitive to the visual and audio signals which the interviewee may give, indicating that he would like to say something. A good way to ensure that these signals are picked up is simply to stop at various places in the interview and ask the employee how he feels about what is being said.

## UNDERSTANDING WHAT THE EMPLOYEE HAS SAID

Yet another of the finer points required for an effective interview relationship is that the interviewer have some idea about what his personal limitations are in actually understanding what the interviewee is saying. The attitude of most people is, "Well, I understand English, what else is there to understanding what an employee says?" The answer to this is "plenty." Effective communication is the subject of entire books. Let's look at several basic things you can do to increase your understanding of an employee.

1. Try to develop or at least assume a stance of being definitely interested in what the person (employee) is telling you.

2. Be aware of the impact that emotionally charged material may have upon you, especially if what the interviewee is saying is making your blood boil.

3. Try to get the gist of what the person is saying and look beyond the facts that he is narrating to you.

4. Don't tolerate or create any distractions. If you can't pay attention to him, don't pretend that you are interviewing him.

5. Try to anticipate what he is going to tell you, as well as what he is telling you, and make an effort to tie the two ideas together with what he has already told you.

If the supervisor makes a real mental effort and concentrates, he will understand the true meaning not only of the words the interviewee says, but also the meaning behind his tone of voice, the gesture of his hands, and the expressions of his face. Without such effort, many cues and warning signals may be completely overlooked by the supervisor. If that happens, of course, the interview will not be as effective as it should be.

## HANDLING RELUCTANT TALKERS

Another of the finer points in establishing a good interview relationship concerns what to do about the person who is disinclined to talk. While it is extremely difficult to make people talk when they do not want to, there are some techniques that may prove useful in encouraging them.

If an employee is reluctant to talk, the interviewer will have to proceed along more structured lines. If the employee is distrustful or bitter, it is sometimes even necessary to tell him honestly why you have to talk to him and why he must talk to you. In all cases, of course, sincere interest in the interviewee as an individual and a genuine feeling of constructiveness about the interview must be in the back of the interviewer's mind.

Sometimes, when everything else fails with the extremely reluctant talker, the interviewer can simply ask the individual why he is reluctant to talk about the subject. This technique often works well, when virtually everything else fails, because it tends, at least, to get the interviewee to talking. Once a person begins to talk, he is more inclined to drop his defensive attitude and continue talking unless he is personally very antagonistic toward the interviewer.

**PART III**     HOW TO GET INFORMATION
               IN AN INTERVIEW

# Chapter 6    How to Be an Active Listener

Gathering information in an interview need not be a difficult task. However, it does take a certain amount of skill by the interviewer. Most of the books and articles written on the subject have one major fault: they encourage the manager to engage in extended periods of discussion with the employee to find out a rather minimal amount of useful information. Usually the techniques recommended require an expenditure of time out of proportion to the value of the information gathered. They not only encourage prolonged discussion but they fail to recognize that many managers are better talkers than listeners.

Any good advice on how to gather information in an interview must enable the manager to avoid wasting an undue amount of time with the employee. We must keep in mind two particular facts: (1) Most people talk far more than they listen, and (2) anyone can be an active listener. Studies substantiate the fact that the average supervisor, while gathering information, will talk up to 85% of the time. Although they do talk most of the time, *they don't think they do.* One study disclosed that a group of managers who had, in fact, talked 90% of the time, felt they talked no more than 50% of the time.

It would appear, then, that the average supervisor is inclined to talk too much. There are many reasons for this. Most of us like to hear our own voices, and we feel that we have something to say. In the interview situation, once a supervisor starts talking, he tends to go on and on, trying to make sure that the person he is attempting to communicate with has the message absolutely correct. Obviously, excessive talking is a detriment to the objective of an information-gathering interview. The supervisor must be aware of the normal propensity of all managers to talk rather than listen.

The second lesson they must learn is to be more active and attentive in their listening roles. Unfortunately, many supervisors are not only overactive as talkers, but they are underactive as listeners, and they are reluctant to improve their listening skills.

## RULES FOR ACTIVE LISTENING

The best examples of how to be an active listener come from those whose job it is to be good listeners—trained psychologists and psychiatrists. They not only give their full attention to the speaker, but they know how to use the questioning technique to obtain deeper and clearer responses from their patients. A list of rules developed from observing their tactics has yielded the following five points that should be useful to supervisors and managers who want to conduct effective interviews:

1. Never be afraid of silence.

2. Be adept at asking encouraging questions.

3. Be encouraging.

4. Use restatement as an active listening device.

5. Summarize what the subordinate has told you.

### Never Be Afraid of Silence

Most people talk too much because they feel uncomfortable when silence prevails. An example of this occurs at small gatherings of people. What happens when there suddenly comes a lull in the conversation? Most people begin to feel uncomfortable, and invariably someone will start talking about something, relevant or not. Furthermore, before someone does get the conversation going again, it is estimated that 90% of the rest of the people in the room are desperately trying to think of something worth while to say, and would make some remark if the first person hadn't already done so.

Abhorrence of silence is unforgivable in a person attempting to gather information in an interview. Visualize a typical interview. A supervisor may ask an employee what he thinks he can do to improve his job performance.

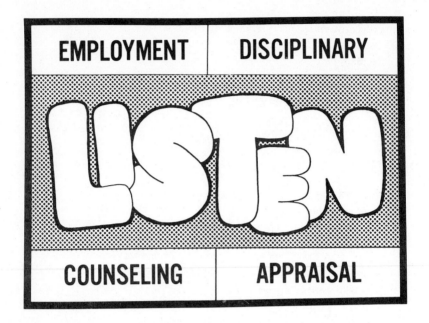

If the employee is unprepared for the question, it may take him a few moments to think of a good, cogent answer. The few moments he takes to organize his thoughts may seem like hours *to the supervisor*. When this happens, the typical supervisor feels a compulsion to say something. If he begins to talk again, the subordinate will forget about finding an answer to the original question. The subordinate won't pursue the original question for a couple of reasons: (1) It is easier to listen to the boss talk than it is to think up a constructive answer to the question, and (2) the boss probably has led the conversation to another subject.

Supervisors must recognize that silence is like a vacuum in that it draws people out, and is thus a tool that supervisors can use. In fact, well-trained interviewers look for "quiet zones" in interviews. They use such periods to organize their own thoughts. The key to using silence as a tool lies in recognizing that long pauses or silent periods need not be embarrassing or awkward. Interviewers simply must avoid "chattering" to fill in silent periods. In short, they should *use* silence, not *avoid* it.

A pause can, in fact, be a decided asset in another way. It can imply that the interviewer is not only interested but expects the employee to contribute something of value. This serves to encourage the subordinate to do his best. Furthermore, a brief lull in the conversation can help to maintain an informal, rather relaxed climate. Often it is after a lull in the conversation that the most meaningful and enlightening information comes forth.

## Be Adept at Asking Encouraging Questions

The second rule for active listening is to be adept at introducing pertinent questions that are designed to encourage the subordinate to talk or divulge information which the supervisor is trying to obtain.

By asking encouraging questions the supervisor is able not only to direct the employee's thoughts towards a specific subject—the employee's performance, a disciplinary problem, a question about how he felt his performance should have been evaluated, or whatever—but he can at the same time place the employee in a position of feeling compelled to speak.

It takes advantage of the psychological point we have just made about the average person's fear of silence. If the supervisor asks a question and then keeps quiet, he can *rely on the fact* that the employee will feel some pressure to talk when *he* is faced by silence. Thus the supervisor may ascertain the employee's ideas and feelings about the situation in question, get the information he desires, and possibly a clue or a suggestion as to what might be done to overcome any difficulty that may exist. An example of encouraging questions are statements such as "Then what . . ." or "Is that so . . ." or "Tell me more . . ."

## Be Encouraging

The third principle of active listening for the supervisor is to let the other person know that you *want* to know what he is talking about. Most people will talk *if* they get attention and interest from the listener. Encouragement, of course, comes from visual as well as oral feedback from the listener. You can encourage the interviewee visually by having an expression of interest on your face, keeping your eyes on the speaker's face, following the animations of the speaker, and so forth. Verbal encouragement is achieved simply by making statements such as "I see . . ." or "Uh-huh . . ." or "Is that so . . ." Brief, interjectory statements such as these tend to encourage the speaker to say more.

An example of how people are compelled to talk by simple encouraging gestures can be readily observed in public places, particularly in public conveyances. Take an airplane, for example, where two total strangers are forced to sit side-by-side for anywhere from one to four hours or more. If one person speaks to the person beside him *and* if the other person "returns" any interest to the person who originates the conversation, they will probably talk during the entire trip. On the other hand, if the person who originally speaks gets no encouraging response from the person toward whom he directed his remarks, they will probably sit side-by-side in silence for the entire trip.

The supervisor interested in getting a person to communicate his ideas to him about a particular subject, should know how to encourage the person to talk both by a visual and by a verbal display of interest. He should cultivate this skill and practice it regularly in interviews.

### Use Restatement as an Active Listening Device

Restating what the other person has just said is another active listening device.

A manager using the restatement technique really needs only to reword or rephrase what the interviewee has just said. Examples of phrases which can be used in restating what someone has said are: "You feel you were fortunate in . . . ," or "You were pretty upset by the fact that . . . ." If the listener "reflects" what the speaker has said by restating it, he can then end his reflection with "Is that correct?"

The supervisor should try to reword or rephrase *as concisely as possible*. This technique has two advantages: (1) The manager clearly establishes *in his own mind* what the subordinate has told him, and (2) the subordinate feels some pressure to elaborate upon any parts which he feels the manager does not understand clearly. He will then attempt to clarify anything which the manager doesn't interpret correctly.

### Summarize What the Subordinate Has Told You

The fifth rule for active listening is: Attempt to summarize the general importance of the ideas and facts which the individual has expressed. Summarizing all that has been said will help to clarify attitudes and overall understanding. It has the added advantage of establishing a basis for further discussion of problems which may have come up. Examples of

summarizing statements are: "These seem to be the main ideas which you have expressed . . ." or "If I understand you correctly, you feel that the situation is . . . ."

The summarizing technique differs from the restatement technique in that the purpose of restatement is to get the subordinate to elaborate on ideas, while the purpose of summarizing is to validate the correctness of the information the supervisor has obtained.  In the restatement technique, the manager may even deliberately misstate information in an effort to stimulate the subordinate to go ahead and talk in more detail about the subject at hand, or at least to reemphasize the correct interpretation of something that has been said.  In using the summarizing technique, the manager should not deliberately misstate factual material, because he is trying to determine whether or not he has correctly received all the information which is available.

# Chapter 7    Asking Questions with a Purpose

Although the discussion on being an active listener goes a long way in helping the interviewer gather more and better information in interviews, perhaps we should discuss in more detail the fine art of asking questions in an interview.

## KEEPING CONTROL

When asking questions in an interview, it is easy to lose control because the person being questioned must be permitted to talk freely. Furthermore, there is sometimes a possibility that the situation will get out of control from an emotional standpoint because the employee may feel he is being "grilled." Nevertheless, the supervisor must maintain control at all times.

Gaining and keeping control in an interview situation is usually easy. Sometimes an interviewer attempts to maintain control by assuming an authoritarian role and making it clear, by either words or action, that he is the boss and the interviewee is the subordinate. This is unfortunate. A supervisor should maintain control over the situation by exerting a conscious alertness to the objectives of the interview and, by asking questions, keep the conversation on the subject. Maintaining control of an interview does not require a person to act like an autocrat nor like an attorney questioning a hostile witness. Nor does it come about simply through using a formal, rigid, structured list of questions. The interviewer should know precisely what information he wants, however, and how he intends to get it.

## RULES FOR MAINTAINING CONTROL WHILE ASKING QUESTIONS

The supervisor who is attempting to get information by asking questions should find the following rules helpful.

1. Always have in mind the general goal of the interview—that is, what information is sought or is to be clarified.

2. Avoid asking questions which have been answered once or which can be answered with a flat Yes or No. Remain alert for evasive tactics.

3. Be flexible in the pattern of conducting the interview. Be willing to allow some free discussion when the prospects seem promising, but be willing to step in and redirect the discussion when the interviewee drifts off the subject.

4. Be courteous and tolerant of interruptions.

5. Allow sufficient time for the interviewee to respond to a question.

6. Be prepared to reword your questions so that the interviewee will know precisely what information is being sought.

7. Be thoroughly acquainted with the facts, situation, or conditions which necessitate the information-gathering interview.

## LEADING VERSUS ENCOURAGING QUESTIONS— A VITAL DIFFERENCE

It was stated above that the interviewer should be adept at asking questions which will encourage the interviewee to talk. However, in an attempt to do so, supervisors sometimes fail because they ask *leading* questions rather than encouraging questions. Leading questions are ones that begin with such phrases as, "Don't you agree that . . ." or "Aren't you in favor of . . . ," and so forth. Any question which begins with a loaded phrase or otherwise inclines the respondent to give a particular answer is a leading question. Such a question almost forces the person to agree with the interviewer, whether or not he does. Therefore, leading questions are of little help in finding out how the interviewee feels or what his thoughts are on a particular subject. They either get a superficial agreement with the statements being made or antagonize the person into forceful opposition.

The real difficulty with leading questions is that many people will agree to almost anything if it is important to them to keep their job or get a job. Leading questions permit them to sense what the interviewer wants to hear, and thus what they should say. The interviewer will not be gathering useful information but hearing only what the person thinks he wants to hear. It is far better for the interviewer merely to be encouraging, making short statements like "I see," or "That's interesting," or "Tell me more about . . . ," and so forth.

One variation of the leading question, which is just as dangerous, is the loaded question. The classic example of the loaded question is "When did you stop beating your wife?" The interviewee will perceive the unfairness of the question and a certain amount of bias on the part of the interviewer. He may not know how to answer the question, he may resent it or, again, he may try to answer it the way he thinks the interviewer wants it answered. Such questions destroy any rapport between the interviewer and the interviewee. The interviewee is apt to feel damned if he does agree or damned if he doesn't. An example of a business-related form of loaded question is: "How long do you expect me to tolerate this kind of performance?" The subordinate simply can't answer this question. Answering the question would force the subordinate into agreeing that he has been performing poorly, or that his poor performance must be tolerated.

Many supervisors do not develop the information they want from an interview. Following a few simple ideas will usually enable the interviewer to get the results he needs.

## WORK FROM GENERAL TOWARD SPECIFIC SUBJECTS

A keystone requirement for successfully gathering information in an interview is having an organized approach to the problem. As a rule, it is good practice to work from a general situation into the specific details which are being sought. For example, when an interviewer is trying to get information about a disciplinary problem, it is a good idea to start talking about general shop conditions and then work into the basic subject of a particular violation of a company rule (or whatever the issue at hand).

Some people argue that working from general to specific subjects is devious, and usually the technique is quickly seen through by the interviewee. The technique has a certain amount of support from a theoretical standpoint, however. In most cases an employee knows beforehand why he is being interviewed. Furthermore, somehow or other, the subject must be broached. There is little to be gained by immediately addressing the subjects. Since the issue cannot be avoided, however, it is probably advisable for the sake of social amenities to work from the general to the specific in getting to the point.

## MAKE EFFECTIVE TRANSITIONS

An invaluable asset in gathering information is the ability to make transitions from one topic to another. Making good transitions requires skill and mental alertness on the part of the interviewer. Experience has shown that being able to change the subject smoothly not only results in getting more information, but it also adds to the pleasure of the interview. Skill at effective transition serves not only to direct the conversation to pertinent areas, but also to bring the discussion back to the issue if it begins to drift. Thus developing this skill is valuable to the supervisor for at least two reasons: (1) it enables him to avoid getting insincere "correct" answers, and (2) it helps him control or direct the interview so that he does get answers to relevant questions.

In a hiring interview, for example, especially if the applicant has had several interviews preceding the current one, he will tend to anticipate the questions and provide pat answers. When the supervisor realizes that he is getting nothing more than standard answers to standard questions, he must be able to change the pace or the sequence of the questions in order to jolt the interviewee out of his complacent attitude. For example, the interviewee may have ready answers to questions such as, "How did you like your last job?", "What were your reasons for leaving?", or "What kind of work would you like to do?" He is probably prepared to tell the story *he* wants to tell by answering these stock questions. However, think how much more revealing his answers might be if the questions were phrased in a different way. The interviewer could ask "What kind of people do you like to work with?", "What did you like the least about your old job?", "Why?", or "What do you think your five most promising talents are, at least so far as our company is concerned?"

By being adept at phrasing good questions and making transitions from one subject to another the interviewer is able to force the interviewee to mentally shift gears, possibly lower his defenses, and do more thinking about the answers he is giving. Keeping the conversation from wandering to irrelevant material may be done by saying, for example, "Let's get back to our discussion of . . ." or "I really think this isn't too important, so let's refer back to . . . ." Guiding the conversation is the supervisor's responsibility. There is no reason why the interviewer should not be frank in expressing the fact that he is not getting the information he wants, particularly if he has established suitable rapport with the interviewee. The interviewer, of course, should be firm but not brusque in bringing the in-

terviewee back to the subject. Sometimes the interviewee is obviously ducking a subject. When this happens, the interviewer's best move is to ask the interviewee point blank why he doesn't want to discuss the subject if he can do so tactfully. An example of how it can be done is as follows: "Why don't you feel that it is important for us to discuss . . .?"

## AVOID DEAD ENDS

Many supervisors find the discussion at a dead end because they ask questions which require no elaboration and no initiative on the part of the person being interviewed. For example, consider what the response is most likely to be when an interviewer says, "George, are you really trying your best out in the shop?" Now think about the same person's response if the supervisor says, "What do you think we can do to help you improve your performance on the lathe?" Question number one will undoubtedly get a brief response, "yes" or "I guess so." However, question number two should make George realize that his work needs improvement, and give him a chance to explain the difficulty and to suggest some constructive action.

Knowing how to avoid dead-end questions is essential in gathering information in an interview. It is especially critical if the interviewee is noncommunicative or resists saying any more than is absolutely necessary. This situation frequently crops up in disciplinary matters, where the supervisor needs to know what happened and the interviewee feels he would be incriminating himself or others if he talks. In such a case, the best tactic to use is to attempt to make the employee feel that he has the opportunity not only to make himself understood but, through the interviewer, to "make a clean breast of it." It sometimes helps (especially in disciplinary matters) to imply that you, the interviewer, have much of the information that you want, but one should not lie. In all cases an honest and sympathetic approach with the employee is best. Do this in a manner in which you encourage him to go ahead and tell what he knows. The best approach is to suggest that he may as well tell you because you know much of it and that, furthermore, what you don't know you'll probably find out from others. It is important that the supervisor understand that he should not badger or otherwise assume an accusing manner with the interviewee in this situation. When this happens the interviewee often will clam up from fear or worry as to what is going to happen to him.

PART IV    HOW TO GIVE INFORMATION
IN AN INTERVIEW

The ability to give information in interviews is at least as important as the ability to gather information. One function of a supervisor is to serve as liaison between top executives and subordinates. Most interviews, especially disciplinary and appraisal ones, are as much for information-giving as they are for information-gathering.

Fundamentally, there are two approaches to giving information in an interview: In one, the interviewer simply gives the interviewee the necessary information; in the other, the interviewer gets the employee to recognize and appreciate some facts that he already knows. Let us start first with techniques for communicating information.

## FACING FACTS

Before a supervisor can successfully get an idea across to a subordinate, he must recognize that he himself must understand and accept the facts of the situation. He must be aware that any situation is determined by many things, such as the individual supervisor himself, the person who is being interviewed, the objective of the interview situation, and the results expected from the interview. Obviously, if the situation is likely to be unpleasant—for example, if the supervisor must tell someone he is being dismissed—facing the facts requires a certain attitude on the part of the interviewer. However, many times the interview situation can be fun—for example, if the supervisor can tell someone that he is getting a raise—and a different attitude can be displayed. Assuming the appropriate role in an interview is not always easy. No one wants to be considered a bad guy or hard to work for. Telling an employee what is expected of him right after he has been hired for a job is always easy to do. But it is not easy to tell an employee that he is being laid off, to reprimand him for infractions of rules, or to criticize his poor performance. Interviews of this kind are the ones with which most supervisors have difficulty.

## THE NEED TO BE FIRM

No supervisor can long avoid his responsibility to give information to subordinates. He is forced to act as a disciplinarian and convey unpleasant news. He finds the task difficult, and often does it poorly. Let us, therefore, give some attention to the process of how to criticize a subordinate.

The watchwords for constructive criticism of a subordinate's performance are "Be firm." Criticism hurts, and having to discipline a subordinate hurts. Being required to tell a subordinate that his performance has not measured up to expectations is generally distasteful. However, the supervisor cannot avoid his responsibility in these areas.

It sometimes helps supervisors in being firm to recognize that there does exist a *need* for criticism. Nothing, for example, is worse for morale than to have members of the employee group turning in less than a satisfactory job and getting away with it. Such a situation undermines the morale of the good workers. Yet some managers, under the misguided goal of being a "nice guy," strive to maintain a friendly and solicitous atmosphere even with subordinates whose output is less than satisfactory. The result is equivalent to bestowing privileges on the lazy or inept workers. The boss who is reluctant to criticize is accused of running a happiness school. Effective management requires that the boss *level* with subordinates, making clear his feelings of dissatisfaction. Obviously, this must be done in a tactful and diplomatic way. The supervisor should keep in mind that "a boss who tries to become well liked by doing favors will not only *not* be well liked, but will also be unsuccessful as a boss."

## GUIDELINES FOR GIVING INFORMATION

Ostensibly, all that is required for a supervisor to give information to a subordinate is an outline, either mental or written, of what information is to be conveyed. It would seem that all he must do is express the information in a way the subordinate will understand. The fact is that many supervisors, even with formal outlines of the information to be imparted,

do the job poorly. They may establish a poor interview relationship with the subordinate or they may be reluctant to impart negative information. The following guidelines should be useful to supervisors who are conducting information-imparting interviews:

1. *Determine what will make a good opening* for the interview.

2. *Keep the discussion above a personal plane at all times.* Recognize that you want to correct a situation, remedy a problem, or give out some facts, not change a personality.

3. *Stick to the facts of the situation.* While it is acceptable to let the conversation drift to a certain extent, an information-imparting interview is not the place for extensive small talk.

4. *Avoid any cross-examination* either by the interviewer or by the interviewee. The situation should not deteriorate into an accusatory or argumentative session.

5. *Free exchange of information is important,* however. The interviewee does have the right to ask questions in an effort to have a point clari-

fied or to shed light on information which may not have been brought to the attention of the interviewer.

6. *Have in mind a clear idea of what the interviewee must learn from the interview* and what results are expected from the interview.

7. *Avoid trying to be funny,* at least if the interview has negative dimensions. While there is a place for humor, attempts to "laugh it off" usually have the effect of watering down the seriousness of the situation and antagonizing the interviewee. Humor can be injected into a positive situation in which the supervisor is telling good things to the subordinate.

8. *Avoid harping* away or repetition. Nothing is more distasteful to the interviewee than to have everything presented the same way, or designed to make the same point. Good vocal communication requires variety in delivery.

9. *Keep in mind, and be sensitive to, the feelings of the individual.* Let him know, for example, that no one else will know about the nature of the interview.

10. *Give the interviewee the opportunity to formulate his own plan* as to what he intends to do about a situation, whether it concerns improved performance, for example, or the time he comes to work in the morning.

11. *At the close of the interview try to tie together any loose ends* which may exist, and clarify the conclusions reached, such as the action to be taken, how it is to be done, and so forth. Also, at this point make a quick review to be sure that everything which was to be told the individual, or discussed with him, has been covered or, if not, that a future time has been set when the material can be discussed.

While it is extremely hard to do a bad job of imparting positive information, it is extremely easy to do a poor job of giving negative information to a subordinate. Most of the mistakes committed by the supervisor in making a critique of a subordinate's performance fall into one of several broad categories. The most serious faults are: (1) making promises which may be impossible to keep, (2) giving unwarranted reassurance, (3) soft-pedalling significant issues, (4) being impersonal and apparently unfeeling, (5) giving uncalled-for advice, (6) overemphasizing particular points, (7) digressing, and (8) being a know-it-all. Let us look at each of these in turn.

## MAKING PROMISES THAT CAN'T BE KEPT

One problem the supervisor needs to avoid is that of making promises to the subordinate which are unwarranted and may not be kept. Leading a subordinate to believe that he will get a promotion when, in fact, no promotion is in sight is an example of this unwise procedure. Other such promises might be telling a subordinate that a bad job by him will be "stricken from the record" when there is no chance that this will happen. Such promises eventually demoralize the employee and lead to a lack of credibility and the deterioration of the superior-subordinate relationship.

## GIVING UNWARRANTED REASSURANCE

When a supervisor, in an effort to minimize the negative impact of a critique session, gives unwarranted reassurances to a subordinate, he is doing the subordinate an injustice. For example, the supervisor shouldn't tell a subordinate that although there is some talk about a reduction in force, he need not worry about it because the supervisor thinks it will all blow over. This kind of talk may be kind and reassuring, but it is irresponsible. The situation will be doubly difficult for both men if the employee does get a layoff. A supervisor who thinks he can get away with minimizing or ameliorating negative circumstances which are going to occur will lose the trust and confidence of all his subordinates, let alone the one who has been led down the primrose path.

## SOFT-PEDALING SIGNIFICANT ISSUES

Some supervisors soft-pedal negative issues in an effort to soften the blow received by the subordinate. While it may be considered kind and humane to try to minimize the impact of negative words, something is lost by glossing over the negative situation and minimizing the impact of the idea. The supervisor should not merely dump the bad news on the employee, but neither should he unduly water down bad news so much that it is not recognized as such by the interviewee.

## BEING IMPERSONAL

Some supervisors, when being critical, are unduly objective and apparently unfeeling in their relationship with the interviewee. They deliberately project a cold, aloof, "all businesslike" image. Many supervisors resort to this kind of "sterile" approach in an effort to cut short the face-to-face confrontation. The idea appears to be that discouraging the subordinate will prevent his asking questions, taking issue with various points, and so forth. While one should avoid *arguing* with the subordinate, there is no excuse for being inhumane in one's approach.

## GIVING ADVICE

Many supervisors, especially in negative situations, are tempted to add their own opinions about matters beyond the scope of the work situation. Invariably, the best advice to these advice-givers is "Don't give it." Even if it is offered with sincere goodwill, it can frequently do more harm than good. Consider, for example, what happens in a *positive* interview if a supervisor advises a subordinate, upon hiring him, to buy a home. The subordinate may follow the advice, buy a house, and two days after clos-

ing the deal have his home washed away in a flood.  Of course, the subordinate didn't have to take the supervisor's advice in a matter not concerned with job performance, but consider the pressure the subordinate
may have felt to buy a home in a particular area once the advice was given.
Would it be surprising if the subordinate never thought much of the supervisor after that time?

## OVEREMPHASIZING AND HARPING

Another difficulty which can occur in an information-giving interview is
the harping away on a particular point, problem, or deficiency which the
superior perceives in the subordinate.  While it is important to emphasize
some points, repeated referral to a particular problem or incident will dis-
courage the interviewee.  In some situations, however, such as when in-
doctrinating a new employee into an organization, repetition may be
advisable.  It does serve the purpose of helping the interviewee get the
whole message and it does reinforce the idea.  In situations where it is
important that the employee get the message right, it sometimes is neces-

sary to state the information in a couple of different ways. However, when repetition becomes harping, it defeats its own purpose.

## DIGRESSING

While it is sometimes revealing to allow a person to follow his own train of thought and wander from the subject to some extent, it is usually not advisable. The supervisor should not permit himself or the other person to waste time. Sometimes, of course, when there is real give-and-take, the main drift of the interview will be sidetracked for a few moments. However, for the most part, the interviewer should consciously stick to the subject and not waste his time *or the interviewee's time* by talking about irrelevant material. Not only does digressing waste time, but it also waters down the importance of the main message, sometimes to such a point that the interviewee doesn't even know what the main message is. In telling a person how to find Interstate Highway 44 from the center of town, it is totally beside the point to explain the architectural design of a building which he will see on the way. You need only say, "You turn left at the corner of 22nd and Pearl."

## BEING A KNOW–IT–ALL

In the information-imparting interview situation, especially when it is in the nature of a critique, the interviewer should not take the position of being a know-it-all. While supervisors should know what they are talking about, they are not omniscient. It is a common human failing that a person who has become an expert in one field will feel that he is all-knowing about almost anything, anywhere, from how to run a drill press—which is the work of the subordinate—to the intricacies of waste disposal in space travel. When a supervisor is tempted to offer guidance to a subordinate on matters not pertaining to the specific company and specific job in question, he runs the risk of playing God. The supervisor must also guard against being impressed with the power he has over the subordinate. Even though the supervisor may feel that what he thinks is right and more important than what the subordinate thinks, the supervisor must not draw unwarranted conclusions. He must be wary of making categorical statements about what the subordinate must do under any circumstances.

## CHECKING THE ACCURACY OF INFORMATION GIVEN

One other point must be made clear in talking about errors committed in information-giving interviews. The supervisor should verify in some way that the interviewee has accurately received the necessary information. Some sort of test must be made, but obviously not a paper-and-pencil kind of exam.

One way to check with him on the important items is to summarize what has been said. Another way is to have the subordinate repeat, in capsule form, the necessary information. Since asking the subordinate to repeat is demeaning to the employee, most supervisors who possess tact and diplomacy avoid this practice. What they usually do is ask whether or not point so-and-so or points $x$ and $y$ are clear, and they themselves do a summary of the major points if it seems necessary.

# Chapter 11　The Difficulty in Attempting To Get People To Use Information They Already Have

Many people have trouble utilizing knowledge they already have. Thus one serious problem in interviewing is getting an employee to recognize that he would have his own solutions to problems if he would only perceive the situation differently. It takes skill to get the subordinate to think for himself and to see that he has sufficient information to answer his own questions. Furthermore, there are other difficulties which crop up in trying to get an employee to recognize that he already has information which he should go ahead and utilize. The supervisor's work is often made difficult because there are mental blocks created by the existence of the superior-subordinate relationship. These problems will be considered in this chapter.

## THE PROBLEM WITH TRYING TO MAKE THE EMPLOYEE RECOGNIZE WHAT HE ALREADY KNOWS

Frequently the boss, in attempting to get an employee to recognize that he has at his disposal information which he should use, runs afoul of one fundamental difficulty in communication. It is very hard to convince anyone that circumstances aren't as he perceives them. Most people are convinced that their own outlook is correct. Any good book on counseling will clearly state that telling, giving orders, and making threats—or admonishing an employee to "use his head" and recognize that the situation is different—simply does not alter human behavior in any significant degree. Admonitions may cause an employee to do something—or not do something—in the immediate future. However, over the long run, orders and threats will not change behavior. Given time, an employee will feel that the person telling him what to do is misinformed, biased, or otherwise not aware of the "real problems" which he is facing and will thus reject the advice.

## FALSE PERSUASION

Sometimes a manager, in trying to get the employee to use information which is already available to him, attempts to *persuade* the employee to recognize the facts as the supervisor sees them. Persuasion probably gets better results than admonition, but it too has its difficulties. The problem with attempting to persuade a subordinate to recognize and discover information for himself is that subconsciously the subordinate may build a mental block against accepting what the manager says. This sometimes happens because there is the implication behind the persuasive effort that the employee is, or at least has been, too stupid to figure things out for himself.

## PROBLEM THAT THE BOSS IS THE BOSS

Because the supervisor holds the position of authority over the subordinate, a status differential automatically influences their relationship. The subordinate may feel a bit reluctant to disagree with the boss in any way, or to "tell on himself." As a result, many subordinates "play dumb" in an effort to act as though certain information were not available to them or, if it were, that there was a logical reason for their not seeing how to use this information.

## SUPERVISORY INTEREST IN EMPLOYEE PERFORMANCE

Another factor in counseling sessions is that the boss has a stake in the outcome of the subordinate's performance. This interest in the same goal should cause a certain amount of rapport between the supervisor and the other person. The subordinate should recognize that supervisors have a personal stake in making sure a subordinate gets the information correctly and performs well on the job. On the other hand, however, this relationship does not guarantee that the superior and his subordinates will work things out. Many people have mental blocks and hang-ups, their minds wander, they are inattentive, or they are just plain forgetful. As a result, they often fail to get all the information, get it correctly, and remember

it. The supervisor himself may push too hard for the subordinate's acceptance of ideas or advice, or he may reject summarily any ideas which the subordinate offers. As a result, the subordinate may feel hurt, get discouraged, and be reluctant to generate his own ideas and utilize the information already available to him.

## THE IMPORTANCE OF INITIATING THE ACTION

Another problem the boss must face in trying to get a subordinate to recognize that he already has certain information which he can use is that the employee himself normally does not initiate the interview. The employee comes to the interview with the idea that he is to be *told* what to do and that little or no input is to be expected from him. More often than not the subordinate looks to the boss for leadership and fails to assume an active role in the situation.

Many people don't like to think for themselves. It is easier to have someone tell them how to correct things than to think about them and make the decisions themselves. And so we have what Professor Jerome C. Darnell refers to as the "no brainer" effect—the idea that most employees don't like to think for themselves and that they will continue doing things the same old (wrong) way unless someone tells them to change.

## MENTAL LOCKING-UP

The final problem which arises in attempting to get an employee to recognize that he should apply some of the information which is available to him is the fact that *even though* the employee may be made to recognize that he is not using the information available to him, he may not change his behavior or performance at work. The hoped-for result of such an information-imparting or counseling session—an improvement in employee behavior—is not going to take place unless the employee *wants* to change his behavior on the job. The employee may have a great deal of insight into what is causing his work to be unsatisfactory, either in terms of performance or discipline, but he still may not change. He may not want to change it or, as happens in some cases, he may not change it simply because he *cannot*. In view of the possible psychological compulsions, the practical supervisor must recognize the fact that some employees do have mental blocks that prevent them from changing their behavior even though they are perfectly aware of what their problem is and even though, physically speaking, they could make the change.

There are three types of employee attitudes toward doing work, the "can do," the "can't do," and the "won't do." When the "won't do" employee is the subject of the interview, no amount of interviewing skill is going to stimulate or motivate the employee toward improved performance. In a case of this kind, the supervisor is justified in taking a very firm and rigid approach—perhaps even a demanding approach—in telling the employee what is what: he may even be justified in firing him.

# PART V    PROBLEM-SOLVING IN INTERVIEWS

## Chapter 12        Handling the Problem-Solving Encounter

Many interviews conducted by supervisors are really problem-solving encounters. There are two ways supervisors can solve problems in interviews: by trial and error or by using insight and intelligence. Obviously, using insight and intelligence is the preferred way to arrive at the right solution. Most books on the subject of solving problems recommend the following procedure:

1. Identify the problem.

2. Determine the causes of the problem.

3. Consider various alternatives which will help resolve the problem.

4. Elect the best or most likely alternative.

5. Implement the one which is considered the best solution.

6. Follow up and be sure that the solution has worked.

The trouble with the above list is that it is good advice only for unilateral problem-solving. When a supervisor can sit at his desk and determine what the problem is, what the various alternative solutions are, and so forth, he is in a situation to implement what he considers to be the best solution. Unfortunately, however, many problem-solving situations are not quite so simple. For example, a supervisor may determine the best answer to the problem of what he will have for lunch—he wants either a salami sandwich and coke or a hot roast beef sandwich and coffee. But he may have more difficulty in determining the best answer to the problem of scheduling overtime, vacations, and so forth. The solutions in cases like these concern other people and are far more complex. The other people concerned have their own personal opinions as to what is best. Thus, the supervisor might determine that the best schedule would have George taking his vacation from June 10th to June 24th, and Al taking his the two weeks beginning June 24th. Unfortunately, however, George and Al may not agree with this decision. Thus problems emerge when the problem to be solved concerns people as well as production. Because supervisors deal with human beings two kinds of problem-solving situations develop. The solution in the first instance, the "supervisory quality" decision, can be based solely upon the judgment of the supervisor and his knowledge of what is required on the job. The solution in the second case, the "employee acceptance" decision, must be influenced by the feelings of the people involved, feelings which may have little or nothing to do with job requirements.

Figure 12.1 illustrates the four problem situations that can derive from the two fundamental types of decisions to be made. All are a function of either the degree of managerial expertise or *quality* required in the decision (indicated by the letter Q) or the degree of *worker acceptance* required (indicated by the letter A).

As can be seen in Fig. 12.1, block 1, there is one kind of situation where the problem to be solved is a high quality problem in which the employee's acceptance of the decision is of little or no importance. Examples of situations such as these involve decisions concerning the introduction of a new product, whether or not to build a new plant, how to finance plant expansion, and so forth.

At the other extreme, indicated by block 4, Fig. 12.1, is a high acceptance situation with low quality overtones. Decisions which are by nature high acceptance but low in quality are those concerning such decisions as who gets the desk by the window or who gets to go on coffee break first. In short, high acceptance decisions are those which concern people and people's feelings; high quality decisions are those which concern managerial expertise.

Obviously, there is a situation wherein the decision to be made is both high in quality and acceptance, as indicated by block 2, Fig. 12.1. Situations like this occur when the managers are considering questions such as whether or not to move a plant from one location to another two miles away. Obviously, such a matter contains grave overtones from the standpoint of the company in terms of financial implications, convenience of customers, accessibility to transportation, and so forth. But there are also grave implications for the company's employees. People are going to be affected because the new location may be closer to or farther from their homes or parking areas, or more or less convenient to public transportation. Some people may not like the new location because they won't be able to ride to work with their neighbor, and so forth. Thus decisions such as one involved in moving a plant contain both a high quality and a high acceptance feature.

Finally, of course, there is the situation in which both the quality and the acceptance of the decision are basically unimportant, and no real problem is present.

## THE POWERFUL IMPACT OF OBJECTIVES

Whenever the question in an interview situation is one of resolving problems, it is extremely important to know what the objectives of the situation are. If a problem is important *only* from a managerial standpoint—a high quality, low acceptance decision—the supervisor can make the decision based upon his own knowledge. Such problem-solving situations do not directly affect the employees, and the only responsibility the super-

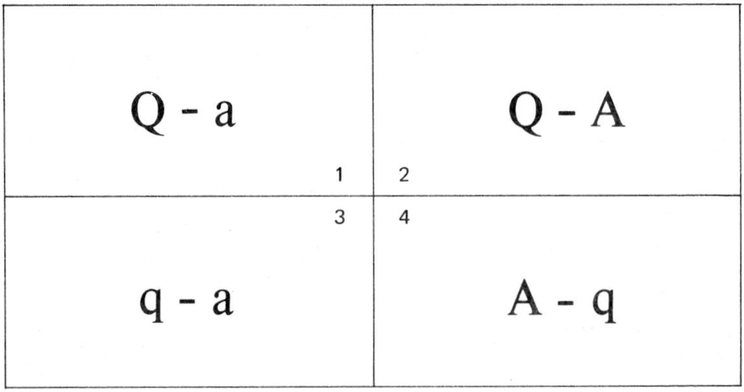

| Q - a | Q - A |
|---|---|
| 1      2 | |
| 3      4 | |
| q - a | A - q |

Q = Quality

A = Acceptance

Figure 12.1

visor might have is to impart information. Decisions in these cases require the open and free flow of ideas only among the experts in whatever field of operations is affected.

The rub comes when the problem involves a high acceptance decision. In these situations it is just as necessary that the supervisor find out what the *feelings* of his people are as it is that they find out what the actual facts of the situation happen to be. That is, when a problem contains a high acceptance aspect, the supervisor must consider the feelings and emotions of people as well as the other facts of the situation. The supervisor must remember that people's behavior is a function of two inputs: the facts of the situation and their attitude toward these facts. Practicing supervisors have found that even when you *change* the facts, behavior will not change unless you can cause a change in employees' attitudes. Indeed, in our society we have a little jingle which attests to the importance of people's attitudes in determining behavior. It says: "Don't confuse me with facts, my mind is made up." Thus the supervisor must ascertain both the real facts and the attitude "facts" to be able to resolve the problem adequately.

## GIVING DIRECTION TO THE PROBLEM-SOLVING INTERVIEW— GUIDED VERSUS UNGUIDED TECHNIQUES

The guided interview has a definite pattern and in general it tends to follow an established procedure or outline. Conducting a guided interview has the advantage not only of working with a structured interview situation, but also of pushing matters through to a predetermined conclusion.

In contrast, there is the unguided interview. In the unguided interview, the participants are usually permitted to ramble along. It is presumed that the conversation will be relevant to the problem at hand. Contrary to what one might think, the unguided interview is probably the better technique in problem-solving encounters. The reason is that many times supervisors are not really aware of the causes of the problems until they get involved in the interview itself. Frequently, what happens is that a supervisor knows that there is a problem—for example, two employees are not getting along well together—and that something needs to be done about it. But he doesn't know what the cause of the problem is. Therefore, he may start off by trying to gather information. He does this by asking questions to determine what the particular subordinate or group of subordinates feel about a certain situation. Thus anything the subordinates say in response to the questions may be relevant.

After a short time he may accumulate enough information to form some idea of what is at the base of the difficulty. At this point in time, the supervisor can shift to a more structured approach *if* the problem is a high quality type. However, if the problem is a high acceptance type, the supervisor must be able to continue on an extremely loose and unguided basis. He simply will not have had time to prepare a formal structure or guideline of questions.

The successful problem-solving interview, therefore, requires a great deal of finesse and capability on the part of the supervisor. He must know how to make transitions from one point to another, be aware when the conversation is drifting from relevant to irrelevant matters, be especially attuned and alert to the sensitivities and feelings of individuals, and understand when a sound agreement is being reached. In short, the supervisor must maintain control of the interview at all times and know when and how to close the interview situation for action results. Let us, therefore, now look at how a supervisor, in either a guided or unguided interview situation, wherein a problem must be solved, can maintain control of the situation and close the interview effectively once the information has been revealed and a solution has been found.

# Chapter 13    Coping with Hostility in Interviews

One of the primary difficulties in maintaining control over an interview or over a meeting of several individuals is caused by overt or subconscious hostility. Unless everyone is in complete agreement with the first idea expressed, there will be disagreement. As a result, an important technique for the supervisor to acquire is the ability to overcome hostility when it occurs, either in a two-person situation or in a group situation.

## OVERCOMING HOSTILITY

Since discussions on such subjects as disciplinary matters, work improvements, grievances, and so forth, are apt to arouse feelings of tension, hostility, and disagreement, a supervisor should expect and be prepared to deal with such emotions. The important thing is not that the supervisor be able to *limit* disagreement and hostility so much as it is that he be able to *control* it when it occurs. The interviewer is in charge of the interview situation; it is up to him to exercise the controls. He must know what to say, how to say it, and when to say it. Furthermore, he must know when to listen. Most importantly, he must know how to guide the conversation away from petty, fruitless arguments into the constructive use of emotions and ideas. If he can capitalize on understanding the thought behind various emotions and ideas, he will ultimately develop insight and intelligence and be able to resolve various kinds of problems.

Basically, the hostility encountered in any interview relationship may be covert and silent or it may be open. The supervisor should be capable of handling either.

## Silent Hostility

Silent hostility—against you personally, fellow-workers, or the company—
is the more difficult type to handle because it is not easily recognized
and it is sometimes misinterpreted. How does one handle the employee
who will not communicate his hostility, but rather lets it seethe inside
him? There are many guidelines which the practicing supervisor should
use in attempting to cope with this situation:

1. Recognize when an employee is disaffected or alienated. One of the
   first things which the supervisor must understand however, is that
   the employee may not necessarily be against him even though he is
   certainly not with him. The supervisor must spot trouble and take
   action as quickly as possible.

2. Encourage the employee to open up, to express his point of view so
   that you can discover what the real problem or source of the hostility
   is. You may have to ask him a point-blank question, such as "Bill,
   I sense you don't agree with what I'm saying. Would you mind telling
   me why?" Such questions usually will make the individual open up
   and give his point of view. The supervisor (and others in the group
   if it is a group discussion) may discover the roots of his hostility. If
   the hostile employee's feelings are not brought out, an effort may be
   made to push the hostile individual into agreement. Such efforts
   usually fail.

3. Try to summarize the points of disagreement. Listening to opposing
   ideas with respect and then giving a summary should make it clear
   what points of disagreement should be pursued before a conclusion
   is reached.

4. The last step in handling the hostile, silent employee is to build pa-
   tiently an atmosphere which will convey to him a feeling of being a
   member of the group. If the subordinate does not want to talk, he
   should not be forced to. However, the point should be made that by
   remaining silent he is not contributing to the problem-solving situation; he may, in fact, be aggravating the situation. If the supervisor
   is inept at sensing when a subordinate is fundamentally hostile or if
   he lacks the skill necessary to draw the individual out, the silent,
   hostile person may scuttle the entire problem-solving encounter.

## Open Hostility

Open hostility is far more easily dealt with than silent hostility. Most supervisors can cope with a situation in which an employee is sounding off, is saying that he disagrees and why, even if his reasons are unsound. The best way to handle open hostility is to be an active listener, to hear the employee out, allow him to ventilate his emotions and feelings, and then get the conversation on a constructive keel by discussing the specific points of disagreement. Obviously, if the person is extremely obstinate, or if there is a polarized point of view, the problem will not be easily resolved. But nevertheless, if people are willing to communicate and talk openly about points of disagreement, things will probably work out to the advantage of all. In this kind of problem-solving situation, the supervisor's chief function is to keep the discussion on relevant issues, keep personalities out of any accusations or hostilities expressed, and concern himself with resolving the major issues of disagreement.

# Chapter 14    Handling Disagreement

How disagreement is handled determines the success of any interview. There are, of course, ways to disagree with people effectively. Furthermore, there are also ways to use disagreement in achieving a cooperative attitude, whether or not ultimate agreement is ever reached.

In handling a situation in which people are disagreeing, the supervisor must recognize that rarely is anyone absolutely right or absolutely wrong. The supervisor should control anyone—including himself—who may begin to make matter-of-fact statements that someone is wrong or someone else is right. Rather, he should evaluate who made the assertion that someone is wrong and why he said it. Making such an assessment usually will go a long way toward guiding the supervisor as to how to handle the situation.

Second, in controlling a situation in which disagreement is voiced, neither the supervisor nor anyone else should attempt to convince anybody that a given position is right. Rarely, at the point of disagreement, does anyone capitulate and say, "I see the error in my thoughts." The wise supervisor will try to provide a face-saving way out for an individual, if he is obviously wrong, or at least an easy way for the individual to accept the fact that it would be logical for him to change his mind.

The third point which should be recognized by the supervisor is that, when disagreement does occur, there are times when no agreement will be reached as a result of the conversation. The supervisor should know when to close the discussion and go on to other problems. Many times during the passage of a little bit of time between the time when a problem comes up and when it is discussed, the antagonists can find points of reconciliation. In the passage of time, people have an opportunity to re-think positions and ideas. Many conflicts can be resolved without obvious effort on the part of the supervisor, or even by his attempting to act behind the scenes.

Probably the key point for the supervisor to remember in attempting to handle a situation where people disagree is that, above all, he should avoid giving the impression that he feels that anyone is all right or all wrong, and that there is no in-between. The supervisor, of course, should not give the impression that he thinks someone is right if he feels the person is wrong, but he should also not give the impression that a person could not possibly be mistaken. Rather, he should leave the matter on a fairly open basis, in which everyone recognizes the fact that there is a point of disagreement, that a solution or a point of middle ground can be reached, and that it will take cooperation among the number of people involved to reach that point of middle ground.

## CHALLENGING A STORY

Once in a while, of course, it is possible in an interview that someone may make a boldfaced assertion which is wrong, or a lie, or at least an exaggeration of the truth. If that assertion, unchallenged, will be detrimental to solving the problem, he must not be permitted to get away with his story. Challenging of a story which someone has manufactured can be extremely touchy. But it is a job that the supervisor must be prepared to do if it becomes necessary.

Fundamentally, the best way to handle a distortion of facts or a lie is to confront the individual making the assertion with open and frank disbelief. There are, fortunately, many ways to confront the employee with the fact that you do not believe his story without saying, "You're a damn liar." Phrases you can use in such circumstances are: "Tell me more, this is extremely interesting to me, for I had heard it differently from someone else," or, "Are you sure you couldn't be mistaken? After all, I had the feeling that . . . ." The way to handle a situation in which a subordinate is fabricating, lying, or distorting the facts deliberately is to let him know that you are not going to let him get away with telling a story, but at the same time give him a face-saving way to get out of the situation.

Sometimes, of course, the employee will not retract the statement that he has made. In this situation it is a good idea not to pursue the issue, but to go on to something else. However, when the subject is dropped, the supervisor should be very careful not to imply in any way that he is accepting the story. He might say simply, "Well, let's drop the subject, we can come back to it later, after we have had time to do some more investigation of the facts." Accusing a person of lying is not recommended; it usually forces him to crystalize his position and, if at all possible, he will deny the truth to his dying breath.

The supervisor must also be prepared for the situation when an employee does back down from an untenable position or story. When this happens, unless the issue which was distorted is a critical one, the matter should be dropped and the correct information accepted at face value. It is poor policy for a supervisor to pursue the fact that a man has lied or exaggerated, and if it is done in front of other people, it may become demoralizing to the individual. Embarrassment and ego damage can result even if others are not present to observe the person's debasement. Furthermore, making an issue of the fact that someone has changed his story would result in a battle of personalities and points of reference and would serve little purpose in addressing the problem which is to be resolved.

## AVOIDING SORE SUBJECTS AND SACRED COWS

All people have emotional hang-ups, subjects about which they are sensitive. A supervisor cannot always avoid unknowingly touching on subjects which an individual does not want to discuss or which may trigger an emotional outburst.

Proper handling of these touchy situations will determine to a large degree the supervisor's success in minimizing the time spent in problem-solving interviews. Many emotional sore spots are caused by worry or fear of various kinds. These fears may concern the loss of a job, fear of being made a fool of, fear of losing status or position, or the fear of emotional hurt (say on racial or religious grounds). Obviously, an interviewer can easily stumble into a situation in which he seems to threaten a person's job, his self-image, or his status in the eyes of other people.

When a supervisor senses that a sore spot has been hit, he should smooth over the situation as quickly as possible, go on to other matters, and let the subject drop. A mistake that many supervisors make in such situations is to attempt to correct what he has said. Such efforts practically always only aggravate the situation and heighten the emotions. For example, in an interviewing situation where reference was made to the fact that a subordinate was found derelict in his duty a year before, it would be unwise for the supervisor to say, after stumbling into the subject, "George, we all know that a year ago you fouled up that project, but we are all understanding and don't hold it against you." Obviously, making a point of the issue, openly recognizing it, and indicating "forgiveness" of it is ridiculous. This simply serves to focus attention on the fact that an unfortunate situation did occur. When a supervisor realizes that he has stumbled upon something with which the employee has a strong ego involvement, he should go on to a different subject. After all, the purpose of the interview is to arrive at a solution of a current plan or action, not to embarrass people. Nothing is gained by resurrecting previous sins of omission or commission unless the facts are necessary in a disciplinary case.

The interviewer is, therefore, well advised to be sensitive to the fact that people are clamming up or otherwise indicating they would prefer not to talk about a particular subject. Especially when the subject is not of prime importance and the person seems reluctant to talk about it, the supervisor should make a transition and move rapidly into another area or drop the subject and say something like "Well, let's look at the problem a different way. It seems that this general approach is not going to be fruitful. Do you have any different ideas as to how we should handle this problem?"

# Chapter 15    Decision-Making in the Interview

In most interview situations a point comes where a decision must be made as a result of the interview. In a counseling situation, a disciplinary interview, an employment interview, an appraisal interview, or an exit interview, something must be decided. What is expected must be defined and a decision made about whether or not to promote or hire a person, or how to improve his performance, what disciplinary action should be taken, or whether constructive changes can be made in hiring or handling personnel.

The decision often lies in the hands of both people involved in the interview. For example, in a counseling interview, it is up to the employee to make a decision as to what he is going to do by way of improving his performance just as much as it is up to the supervisor to decide what is to be done if the employee doesn't. In a disciplinary interview, it is up to the subordinate to decide whether he can or will change his behavior pattern; at the same time, it is up to the supervisor to decide what will be done about the situation in the immediate future. In an appraisal situation, the supervisor will decide whether to recommend the man for a raise, how much pay increase he should get, whether or not to recommend a promotion, and so forth, but it is also up to the subordinate to decide whether the decision fits in with his ideas, goals, and personal objectives.

## THE TWO CARDINAL SINS OF DECISION-MAKING

Making decisions is probably one of the most difficult problems people face, even experienced supervisors. The two primary sins which managers commit when it comes to making decisions are procrastination and vacillation.

### Procrastination

If a person puts off making a decision on a matter he should face up to, he is really making a decision not to decide, which in most cases is the poorest decision in any kind of situation. The problem with procrastination is the fact that no decision is rendered until it is too late or a forced decision is imposed upon the supervisor himself. In either case what is done is not done properly, if it is done at all.

### Vacillation

When a person vacillates, it means that he is unable to decide between two or more alternatives. In this case, as with procrastination, he fails to make a decision or tries to hedge his bets. He puts off or fails to take forthright action.

## HOW TO MAKE DECISIONS AS A SUPERVISOR

Anyone who procrastinates or vacillates is not an effective decision-maker. Besides their personal ambivalence in any given situation, there are many other reasons why people fail to make decisions. Sometimes they can't because they feel they do not have the authority to do so. More commonly, however, they simply lack confidence in themselves. Let us look at some of the recommended guidelines for effective decision-making.

The following basic rules will help a supervisor be effective at making decisions.

1. *Determine what is really important and what is unimportant.* Then don't allow the unimportant matters to concern you at the time of making a major decision.

2. *Where possible, rely on established procedures.* The supervisor need not be unduly rigid in applying policy or standard operating procedures, but he should be aware of what these established procedures are.

3. *Avoid making decisions while under stress.* Obviously, it is sometimes impossible to avoid stress, especially in a rather traumatic situation—

say a disciplinary interview. However, there is no excuse for the supervisor's making a hasty decision when he is under a great deal of pressure. If nothing else, he can get up and walk around the table or simply lean back, close his eyes, and think about the implications of the decision which he is about to render.

4. *Don't try to anticipate everything that can possibly happen as a result of your decision.* Many supervisors worry unduly about what some-one will do as a result of their decision—for example, to lay off a person. Many times they think in terms of what the employee will think, what his wife will think, and so forth. No one can tell what the final result of a particular outcome will be. As we noted in *Managing the Marginal and Unsatisfactory Performer*,* statistics indicate that in all likelihood the man who is fired may be better off than he would have been if kept on a job where his performance was unsatisfactory.

5. *Don't expect always to be right.* Many times people make mistakes and that is to be expected. In fact, most senior executives in large organizations aren't so concerned about being right as they are concerned about not being wrong. The average supervisor feels that if one thing isn't right, it is automatically wrong. This attitude reflects a rather limited outlook. After all, it is not so much a question of being *absolutely right* as it is a question of trying to avoid being *absolutely wrong.* In practically all situations there are numerous ways to make a thing work. Most good decision makers know that whether the decision is absolutely the best possible one is not so important as whether the decision can be implemented and made to work.

6. *Don't be afraid of failure.* Many people hesitate to make decisions simply because they are afraid they won't make the right ones. It would be nice for all of us if we could be sure we'd never make a mistake. The only way of being sure not to make a mistake is not to do anything. The supervisor must not allow himself to be so fearful he hesitates to go ahead with confidence and act on his decisions. As Nicholas Murray Butler, past president of Columbia University, was fond of saying, "There are really only three kinds of people: those who make things happen, those who watch things happen, and those who don't know what happened." Obviously, the most effective supervisor is one who makes things happen, and making things happen means that a person must not be afraid of failing.

---

* Lawrence L. Steinmetz, Reading, Massachusetts: Addison-Wesley, 1969.

7. *"Cultivate decisiveness"* is another good rule for the supervisor to follow. Making a decision and then worrying about how to make the decision work is far more likely to relieve the decision-making tensions involved in an interview situation than worrying about whether one is making the right decision. Subordinates can sense indecisiveness.

8. *Once the decision has been made and the follow-up arranged, forget it.* When a person continually reviews a decision he has made, he actually is engaging in *de facto* vacillation. If a supervisor keeps going back and worrying about whether the decision he made was the right one, he can easily talk himself into changing the decision and various plans. This is almost always poor policy and a waste of time.

9. *Effective decision-makers change decisions, once they are rendered, in only one of three situations:* when they have been proven dead wrong, when they have the opportunity to capitalize on an unforeseen circumstance, or when the means of implementing the decision cannot be worked out. In no other situation should a supervisor change a decision. Keeping this last sentence in mind should help the interviewer be far more forceful in rendering decisions in interview situations or any other time, for that matter.

# PART VI      HOW TO END AN INTERVIEW

Knowing how best to close the interview is an area which in some cases provides problems for supervisors. Usually it is easy to close an interview, especially an information-giving interview. As outlined in Chapter 9, all the supervisor needs to do is double-check that all the information was given and understood by the interviewee. Similarly, as outlined in Chapter 8, it should be easy to close an information-gathering interview because, at some point, it becomes obvious that no more information will be forthcoming. In other situations the supervisor can terminate an interview when agreement has been reached. However, in some situations it is not obvious when "everything has been done." Let us, therefore, look at the critical factors which should be considered for situations in which the point of closure is not clear.

## WHEN TO CLOSE

Setting a time limit or attempting to establish fixed rules about when to close is not a pratical way to handle the situation. The question to answer is "Has the problem been solved to the satisfaction of those concerned or does more work need to be done?" If the situation has been resolved satisfactorily, it is obviously time to close the interview. If, however, additional work is needed, but continuing does not seem productive at this particular time, the interview can nevertheless be brought to a close on a strong positive note by establishing a time to continue discussing the problem.

The decision to close an interview should be made by the supervisor. He can arrive at his answer by asking the question, "Are we *both* ready to close?" Too often, of course, the interviewer is inclined to consider only his own feelings. Many people appear reluctant to close simply because they feel something else needs to be said. Others simply want to go on talking; they feel an obligation to continue talking even when they know they have nothing more to say of any substance. The basic guideline that the supervisor should use should run as follows: The interview should be closed when he feels that further discussion will not contribute any significant information.

## HOW TO CLOSE THE INTERVIEW AND CONSOLIDATE YOUR GAINS

Closing an interview is easy. Simply draw together everything that has transpired and make clear what has been agreed on and what is still to be done. Here is a good guideline to follow, particularly if the interviewer expects to get action of some kind as a result.

1. Summarize the points which were covered and especially the points on which agreement was definitely made.

2. Make clear any action the employee will be expected to make.

3. Make some general statement as to overall evaluation of the success or failure of the meeting.

4. If results are to be obtained and practices implemented, set a time at which progress will be checked.

When the supervisor has gone through all these steps, he will have effectively closed the interview. Then all that is required is a statement of "Let's get back to work."

## THE ADVANTAGE OF A STRONG CLOSE

If making a decision has been part of the purpose of the interview, you should close with an action plan in mind. An action plan should consist of a clear agreement between supervisor and employee as to who is to do what, when he is to do it, what results are expected from the action, and when these results should be evident. This kind of close to the interview gives both the supervisor and the employee a yardstick by which to measure future performance.

## WHY FOLLOW-UP IS NECESSARY

The interviewer's responsibility for an interview does not end with the termination of the interview. He must make an evaluation as to the effectiveness of the discussion and the recommendations or decisions reached. If an action plan has been agreed on, he should keep notes as to who is to do what, and what results are expected, and when. The responsibility of the interviewer does not end until the results come in, and these results are *evaluated and considered acceptable.* If, in fact, at the end of the time established for the results to be in, the results are not satisfactory, the interviewer's responsibility will continue until such time as corrective action is taken and the final results are acceptable.

**PART VII**     HOW TO RATE YOURSELF ON
YOUR INTERVIEWING SKILLS

**Practical Guide and Checklist**
**For Evaluating Your Own Performance**
**As An Interviewer**

---

After you have conducted an interview, a real one or a practice one from the role-playing cases which follow, you can rate your own performance. Answer each question. A perfect paper would contain all Yes answers.

## SECTION 1   THE INFORMATION–GATHERING INTERVIEW

|  | YES | NO |
|---|---|---|
| 1. Did I have a firm idea in mind as to what the objective of the interview was? | ____ | ____ |
| 2. Did I make the purpose of the interview clear to the interviewee? | ____ | ____ |
| 3. Did I indicate to the interviewee where I wanted him to sit, and so forth? | ____ | ____ |
| 4. Were we comfortable in the interview situation, from the standpoint of physical surroundings? | ____ | ____ |
| 5. Were we free from needless interruptions? | ____ | ____ |
| 6. Did I avoid trying to do other things while I conducted the interview? | ____ | ____ |
| 7. Did I have well-prepared introductory remarks? | ____ | ____ |

|  | YES | NO |
|---|---|---|
| 8. Did I try to develop a good atmosphere for the interview? | ___ | ___ |
| 9. Did I establish rapport with the interviewee? | ___ | ___ |
| 10. Did I make an effort to overcome any defensive attitude on the part of the interviewee? | ___ | ___ |
| 11. Did I attempt to talk to him on his level and in terms with which he is familiar? | ___ | ___ |
| 12. Did I instill confidence in the interviewee? | ___ | ___ |
| 13. Did I communicate clearly to the interviewee the ideas that I had in mind? | ___ | ___ |
| 14. Did I listen carefully when he had things to say? | ___ | ___ |
| 15. Did I make an effort to empathize with him? | ___ | ___ |
| 16. Did I avoid over-talking the interviewee? | ___ | ___ |
| 17. Did I give him the opportunity to sound me out? | ___ | ___ |
| 18. Did I avoid making any snap judgments? | ___ | ___ |
| 19. Was I primarily nonjudgmental in my attitude toward the interviewee? | ___ | ___ |
| 20. Did I look for hidden meanings in what he was saying? | ___ | ___ |
| 21. Did I reflect upon what he was telling me during the process of the interview? | ___ | ___ |
| 22. Did I try to give him an opportunity to formulate his own action plan? | ___ | ___ |
| 23. Was I objective in the interview? | ___ | ___ |
| 24. Did I give the interviewee the opportunity to ventilate his feelings and emotions? | ___ | ___ |
| 25. Was I interested in what he was telling me? | ___ | ___ |
| 26. Was I encouraging to the interviewee? | ___ | ___ |

|  | YES | NO |
|---|---|---|

27. Did I use the technique of asking encouraging questions? _____ _____

28. Did I utilize the restatement technique in attempting to get additional information? _____ _____

29. Did I make an effort to summarize what the interviewee had told me? _____ _____

30. Did I work from general subjects to specific subjects? _____ _____

31. Did I do a good job at making transitions from one subject to another, and yet keep in mind the main purpose of the interview? _____ _____

32. Did I avoid asking dead-end questions? _____ _____

## SECTION 2    THE INFORMATION-GIVING INTERVIEW

|  | YES | NO |
|---|---|---|

1. Did I face the facts of the situation? _____ _____

2. Was I firm in my approach? _____ _____

3. Did I establish a good opening for the interview? _____ _____

4. Did I keep the situation above a personal plane? _____ _____

5. Did I stick to the facts of the situation? _____ _____

6. Did I avoid cross-examining the interviewee? _____ _____

7. Did I give the interviewee the opportunity to ask me questions? _____ _____

8. Did I have a clear-cut idea in mind as to what information I wanted to get across to the interviewee? _____ _____

9. Did I try to avoid being funny or flip in a serious situation? _____ _____

10. Did I avoid harping or too much repetition? _____ _____

|  | YES | NO |
|---|---|---|

11. Did I keep in mind the feelings of the interviewee?

12. Did I give the interviewee the opportunity to formulate his own plans?

13. Did I try to gather any loose ends and summarize at the close of the interview?

14. Did I avoid making promises that may not be kept?

15. Did I avoid giving unwarranted assurances?

16. Did I avoid being unduly impersonal in my attitude?

17. Did I avoid giving advice that was not called for?

18. Did I avoid overemphasizing particular points?

19. Did I keep the interview situation from digressing to irrelevant subjects?

20. Did I avoid being a know-it-all?

21. Did I make an effort to check the accuracy of the information with which I started?

22. Did I try to get the employee to recognize his own problems (assuming he should have been able to)?

23. Did I avoid trying to tell the employee things that he already knew?

24. Did I avoid trying to unduly force the employee into accepting ideas?

25. Did I make an effort to be objective?

26. Did I make an effort to overcome the hostility which the interviewee may have had?

27. Did I look for signs that he was not really with me as to what was going on in the interview situation?

28. Did I try to get the employee to open up and give his point of view?

|   | YES | NO |
|---|---|---|

29. Did I make an effort to draw out points of disagreement between the interviewee and myself?

30. Did I try to build an atmosphere of teamwork?

31. Did I avoid openly putting down the employee?

32. Did I avoid pulling rank to make him accept my
ideas?

33. Did I tactfully let the interviewee know he couldn't
get away with telling "stories"?

34. Did I adequately handle the discussion of sore
subjects?

35. Did I close the interview firmly, reviewing an action
plan to which we both had agreed?

36. Did I avoid procrastinating or vacillating when I
should have made the decision?

# PART VIII  ROLE-PLAYING CASES FOR PRACTICE INTERVIEWS

## INSTRUCTIONS FOR ROLE-PLAYING
## THE PRACTICE INTERVIEWS

The following cases provide role-playing situations. *Role playing* is a technique in which people learn about a case by assuming the various roles involved and acting them out, rather than merely reading about and discussing the situation.

Stated simply, the way these role-playing cases are to be used is as follows: Each case will contain a statement describing the general circumstances of the case. This is labeled *The Situation* and is to be read to all participants.

Each case next has a section on the *Requirements of the Situation.* This section of the case will instruct the leader of the training session as to how many role players are required in the case, and how the case is to be conducted. This section, too, can be read to all trainees.

The third section of each case is entitled *Specific Instructions for . . . .* This section will contain the specific instructions to be given to each role player. Note that these instructions are given only to the people playing the role and any observers. They are *not* given to other role players (otherwise the others would know what to ask for).

The last section of each role-playing case is entitled *How to Critique the Case.* This section contains information regarding the conduct of the case, the information which should have been developed from playing the roles, and other guidelines as to how to evaluate the various role-players' performances. The trainer uses this section to critique the trainers (and to instruct anyone who may be observing the training session).

The idea behind using role-playing cases for teaching interviewing skills to supervisors is that role playing provides a realistic situation in which to train. Each participant should assume the attitudes, ideas, and feelings which would represent those of the individual involved in the situation. In assuming these attitudes and feelings, each role player then finds himself in a face-to-face confrontation with a real person who has feelings. The players are required to develop information, ascertain feelings, avoid personality disputes, etc., just as they would in a real-life situation. The advantage of working under these conditions is that if the trainees foul up the process, no harm is done, whereas getting the training on the job can lead to real trouble. In role playing, learning takes place, nevertheless, and the participants can analyze what went wrong, and why and how the difficulties could have been avoided. In short, role playing dramatizes the training situation and helps the trainee not only learn the principles of interviewing, but how to apply them in dealing with problems involving the feelings and opinions of other people.

For convenience to the users, the pages containing case material have been perforated and arranged so that the parts for individual role players can be separated and distributed.

## Case 1

### Conducting a Job Interview
### THE OWENS PRINTING COMPANY

---

**THE SITUATION** *(Read by or to all participants)*

Roger Owens owned and managed the Owens Printing Company which
employed thirteen people. A lack of modern equipment caused severe
problems. He lost many of his clients—particularly the big ones—because
he wasn't able to produce jobs of the size and within the time limit they
wanted.

Owens Printing operated three offset presses and two letter presses. These
machines were outdated. However, standard printing techniques were
used in the operation of these machines. While Owens was not proud of
the equipment in his shop, he was reasonably proud of the quality of the
jobs which he was able to produce. He was particularly proud of the fact
that his people made relatively few errors that would result in increased
cost and inconvenience. As Owens lost business to firms with more modern equipment, he began to compete by specializing on printing high-
quality products with the machinery he had.

One of the real problems in an information-gathering interview—which is
what the problem is in this case—is how to obtain sufficient information
so that a wise decision can be made. In this case we are going to deal with
a job application and decide whether or not to hire this prospective employee. This case underscores many of the problems that can occur in an
employment interview. It concerns Roger Owens's problem in replacing
Larry Stegall. Roger is the president of Owens Printing Company and
Larry Stegall is the plant manager. Stegall has just resigned, giving two

95

weeks' notice to Owens. Burton J. Cohen has applied for Stegall's job. The text of the case gives some background on Owens himself and on the Owens Printing Company.

## REQUIREMENTS OF THE SITUATION

Some one person should be selected to assign the roles, cut off the role-playing at an appropriate time, and lead the discussion and assessment which will follow. The process which should be used in role-playing this case is as follows: At least three people are required, one for the role of Roger Owens, one for the role of Burt J. Cohen, and one or more to be observers. The person identified as Mr. Roger Owens should read all the following material designated as "Specific Instructions for Roger Owens." The person to take the role of Burt J. Cohen should read the material under "Specific Instructions for Burt Cohen." The person playing Roger Owens should attempt to utilize all the information available to him from the case material in deciding whether or not Burt Cohen is a likely candidate for the job as plant manager.

The individual playing Burt Cohen should assume the role of being a serious individual seeking a job as plant manager at the Owens Printing Company. He should assume as fact the information as it appears on the following application form. He may improvise any other information called for in the interview, providing it is consistent with the other statements. He should react to whatever happens in the interview situation according to his own feelings and sensitivities at the time.

## SPECIFIC INSTRUCTIONS FOR ROGER OWENS, Interviewer

Your problem is to find someone to replace Larry Stegall, who has just given two weeks' notice as your plant manager. The following are excerpts, notations, and other in-basket information which you have received over the past couple of weeks.

## EXHIBIT 1.1

ORGANIZATIONAL CHART, OWENS PRINTING COMPANY

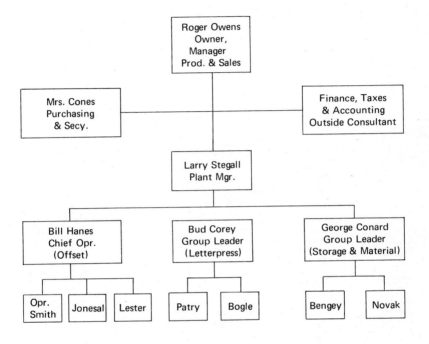

**EXHIBIT 1.2**

Feb. 25

Rog:

The Int'l Rep. from Local 434
dropped by the plant again
Today. He's going to organize
these fellows.
What to Do ?!?

L. Stegall

## EXHIBIT 1.3

Phone call
Thurs., 1:00 p.m.

To:  Mr. Owens

Re:  Application of Mr. Cohen

The Ace Employment Agency phoned while you were
out and I took the following notes from Mrs.
Carter who interviewed him there:

I would say that Mr. Cohen has a great deal of
public relations savvy.

Some people have apparently criticized him as being rather superficial in his behavior, but I
don't get this impression.

He has exceptional ability to present ideas
clearly and convincingly and to arouse enthusi-
asm and support for them.

Has a facility to simplify problems and relationships.

Strikes me as being the type that works hard and
plays hard.

Is exceptionally original and creative in his
thinking.

Makes a tremendous initial impression.

ac

**EXHIBIT 1.4**

## APPLICATION FOR EMPLOYMENT

(Use Pencil or Typewriter)

NOTE: Applications will be kept active for one year

TEST CARD SENT _____ DATE _____

**Name** (As shown on Social Security Card)
(Print) (Last) COHEN (First) BURTON (Middle) J.

Social Security Number 444-38-3960

**Local Address** 112 SO. ROSTO DENVER
Telephone 636-9693

**Other Address** _____ Telephone _____

**Date of Birth** SEPT. 26, 1938

Single ☐  Engaged ☐  Married ☐  Widow(er) ☐  Separated ☐  Divorced ☐ — Married ☒

**Height** 6'0"  **Weight** 178  **Number of Dependents** THREE  **Ages of Children** 8, 6

**Physical Limitations?** NO (Explain on back)
**Have you received injury compensation?** NO
U.S. Citizen YES  Military Status DISCHARGED (HON.)

**Any medical or psychiatric treatment during the past five years?** NO
**Have you been arrested, for other than traffic violations?** YES

**Name of Wife or Husband** MARY  His-Her Occupation HOUSEWIFE
**Where Employed** _____

**How long do you plan to work** PERMANENTLY
**Date Available** IMMEDIATELY

**TYPE OF WORK DESIRED**
1. FOREMAN, PRINT SHOP  2. _____  3. _____
Full Time X  Part Time _____  Permanent _____  Temporary _____  Hours Can Work AS REQ'D

**PREVIOUS EMPLOYMENT** (List most recent job first - include military service)

**Name of Employer** CARLSON, INC.
**Street** 18TH & LARIMER
**City** _____
**Name of Supervisor** AL CARLSON
Employed From 1969 To DATE
Job Duties SHOP FOREMAN PRINT SHOP
Monthly Pay 850/MO.
Reason for Leaving DISLIKED HOURS

**Name of Employer** TIDY, INC.
**Street** 14TH & PIDGEON
**City** _____
**Name of Supervisor** JOE SCHWARTZ
Employed From 1966 To 1969
Job Duties PRESSMAN
Monthly Pay 700/MO.
Reason for Leaving BETTER JOB

**Name of Employer** TAB TRUCKERS
**Street** _____
**City** COMMERCE CITY
**Name of Supervisor** MR. MOYERT
Employed From 1964 To 1966
Job Duties TRUCK DRIVER
Monthly Pay 500/MO.
Reason for Leaving DIDN'T LIKE TRUCKING

(Additional employment may be listed on back)

**Relatives Working** Name _____ Relationship _____
Name _____ Relationship _____

**EDUCATION**
Circle highest year completed
Grade 1 2 3 4 5 6 7 8
High School 1 2 3 ④
Business School 1 2
College or University 1 2 3 4
Undergraduate ☐
Major _____
Year Graduated _____
Institution _____
Graduate Degree Mas Doc ☐
Major _____
Year Graduated _____
Institution _____

**OTHER SCHOOLS OR SPECIAL TRAINING**

**TEST SCORES**
Do not write Below
Name _____
Number _____
Problems _____
Vocabulary _____
Filing _____
Spelling _____
Typing Speed _____
Typing Accuracy _____
Shorthand Speed _____
Shorthand Accuracy _____

**SKILLS** (Check)
Duplicating Machines
Adding Machine
Calculator
Key Punch
Tabulating Mach.
Typewriter (Elect)
Typewriter (Manual)
Dictation Machine
Shorthand — any system

**IMPORTANT**
I understand that giving false information is cause for discharge. A loyalty oath and a physical examination may be required.

Signature Burton J. Cohen

**EXHIBIT 1.5**

Feb. 27

Rog:
 I don't know if you're planning to replace me with Burt
Cohen, but you'd better know
his wife is damned un-
happy here in Denver.

L. Stegall

## EXHIBIT 1.6

Notes taken from telephone reference check with Mr. Al Carlsen, previous boss of Burt Cohen:

Burt's relationships with people are warm and friendly.

At times it appears that Burt is somewhat indecisive and unwilling to assume risks. I wonder sometimes if a great deal of his effectiveness is due to his ability as a failure-avoider.

He has the ability to come up with fresh and original ways of thinking about and doing things.

He is able to visualize things in perspective and goes immediately to the heart of problems.

He is not afraid to give people their head. He gives good people room to move.

I have seldom seen him in the shop after hours. If one didn't know better, he would think Burt was lazy.

Burt is hard for me to figure out. He exhibits no clear-cut managerial personality.

Burt has an extremely happy family life and spends a great deal of time with them.

Burt has high ethical standards and expects others to have the same. If there is anything he gets irritated about, it is when people don't live up to what he expects of them in honesty and moral behavior.

Burt works through conferences with his people. He encourages a tremendous amount of participation.

One of Burt's former instructors told me that he achieved only average grades.

I think Burt kind of leans toward unions.

## BACKGROUND FOR BURT J. COHEN

You are Burt J. Cohen, and you have just applied for a job as plant manager at the Owens Printing Company. You are to assume that all the information given on the application form is true. You may fabricate whatever other material is required, providing it is consistent with the information on the application form.* Finally, you *must* assume you want the job.

---

*A duplicate of the application blank is given in Exhibit 1.7, so that Burt Cohen can also have a copy.

# EXHIBIT 1.7

**APPLICATION FOR EMPLOYMENT**                 TEST CARD SENT

(Use Pencil or Typewriter)
NOTE: Applications will be kept active for one year

| | |
|---|---|
| Name (Print) (Last) COHEN (First) BURTON (Middle) J. | Social Security Number 444-38-3960 |
| Local Address 112 SO. ROSTO DENVER | Telephone 636-9693 |
| Other Address | Telephone |

| Date of Birth 26 SEPT. 1938 | Single ☐  Engaged ☐ | Married ☒  Widow(er) ☐ | Separated ☐  Divorced ☐ |
|---|---|---|---|

Height 6'0"  Weight 178   Number of Dependents NO   Number of Children FOUR   Ages of Children 8, 6

Physical Limitations? NO (Explain on back)   U.S. Citizen YES   Military Status DISCHARGED (HON.) YES

Any medical or psychiatric treatment during the past five years? NO   Have you been arrested, for other than traffic violations? YES

Name of Wife or Husband MARY   His-Her Occupation HOUSEWIFE   Where Employed

How long do you plan to work PERMANENTLY   Date Available IMMEDIATELY   Hours I Can Work AS REQ'D

**TYPE OF WORK DESIRED**

1. FOREMAN PRINT SHOP  2.  3.

**PREVIOUS EMPLOYMENT** (List most recent job first - include military service)

| | |
|---|---|
| Name of Employer CARLSON, INC. | Employed From 1969 To DATE |
| Street 18TH & LARIMER | |
| City | |
| Name of Supervisor AL CARLSON | |

Job Duties SHOP FOREMAN PRINT SHOP
Monthly Pay 850/MO   Reason for Leaving DISLIKED HOURS

| | |
|---|---|
| Name of Employer TIOY, INC. | Employed From 1966 To 1969 |
| Street 14 IU & PIDDGEON | |
| City | |
| Name of Supervisor JOE SCHWARTZ | |

Job Duties PRESSMAN
Monthly Pay 700/MO   Reason for Leaving BETTER JOB

| | |
|---|---|
| Name of Employer TAB TRUCKERS | Employed From 1964 To 1966 |
| Street | |
| City COMMERCE CITY | |
| Name of Supervisor MR. MOYERT | |

Job Duties TRUCK DRIVER
Monthly Pay 500/MO   Reason for Leaving DON'T LIKE TRUCKING

(Additional employment may be listed on back)

Relatives Working  Name _____ Relationship _____
                   Name _____ Relationship _____

**EDUCATION**

Circle highest year completed

Grade 1 2 3 4 5 6 7 8
High School 1 2 3 ④
Business School 1 2
College or University 1 2 3 4
Undergraduate
Major
Year Graduated
Institution
Graduate Degree Mas Doc
Major
Year Graduated
Institution

**OTHER SCHOOLS OR SPECIAL TRAINING**

| SKILLS (Check) | DATE |
|---|---|
| Duplicating Machines | |
| Adding Machine | |
| Calculator | |
| Key Punch | |
| Tabulating Mach. | |
| Typewriter (Elect) | |
| Typewriter (Manual) | |
| Dictation Machine | |
| Shorthand — any system | |

**TEST SCORES**
Do not write Below

Name
Number
Problems
Vocabulary
Filing
Spelling
Typing Speed
Typing Accuracy
Shorthand Speed
Shorthand Accuracy

**IMPORTANT**

I understand that giving false information is cause for discharge. A loyalty oath and a physical examination may be required.

Signature _Burton J. Cohen_

## HOW TO CRITIQUE THE INTERVIEW

### Results Sought from the Interview

Roger Owens needs further information, of course, from Burt Cohen before he decides whether or not to have him replace Larry Stegall.

Some of the things which should be determined by the individual playing the role of Roger Owens, attempting to decide whether or not to hire Cohen, would include the following:

1. What, in fact, is Cohen's stance on labor unions?

2. Is Cohen a public relations type of individual?

3. Would Cohen be apt to antagonize old customers?

4. Does Cohen's behavior appear superficial and insincere?

5. Would Cohen have a tendency to have too many irons in the fire?

6. Does Cohen present his ideas clearly?

7. Does Cohen have a tendency to oversimplify?

8. Would Cohen be a "work-hard–play-hard" type?

9. Is Cohen creative in his thinking?

10. Would Cohen's managerial judgment be balanced and sound?

11. Would Cohen sustain his initial impression?

12. How important is Cohen's dislike of the hours previously worked, and is he a clock watcher?

13. Does Cohen have a drinking problem?

14. Does Cohen have a history of physical or mental illness?

15. Is Cohen having difficulty at home with his wife?

16. What kind of relationship does Cohen have with other people?

17. Is Cohen indecisive?

18. Would Cohen be a good boss?

19. What qualities *make* a good boss?

In evaluating the role-playing situation, the leader of the group and the observers should note to what extent the player who assumed Roger Owens' position developed clear-cut answers to the questions on page 115. If he has adequately developed information about all these points, he should be in a position to determine whether or not he would offer Cohen the job at this time. He should also be able to explain to the group why he would or would not. He should then be prepared to withstand a critique of his rapport with the person who played the part of Cohen.

## Employment Interview
Mary Jones, Secretary

---

## THE SITUATION *(Read by or to all participants)*

Two people will play this case, Mary Jones and Al Smith, the office manager of Acme, Inc. Al Smith is in need of a secretary. Several girls have already applied for the job, but none seem to meet the qualifications that he has in mind. He has placed ads in newspapers and been in touch with several employment agencies. He is now beginning to feel the pressure of not having had a secretary for two weeks, and he is getting desperate about finding one.

Today, out of the blue, Mary Jones walked in and said that she would like to apply for a job. Al has just had her finish filling out the application (see Exhibit 2.1), and he is preparing to interview her for the job. Mary is attractive, well spoken, and well poised. Al must now determine whether she is the right person for the job.

## REQUIREMENTS OF THE SITUATION

For this case we need only two role players plus a leader and one or more observers. The person who assumes the role of Al Smith will be interviewing; the person who assumes the role of Mary Jones (hopefully, a female employee) will be interviewed. All the material disclosed on the application is to be accepted as accurate. The person playing the role of Mary Jones should act and react as she would naturally in an interview situation, sticking to the facts of the situation as indicated in the application form and improvising whenever necessary. The person playing the role should assume that Mary Jones really wants the job and act as if she were really involved in the situation.

The person playing Al Smith must assume that he is trying to hire a secretary for his company. He should, therefore, apply the usual tests given applicants for the position, and should see that she meets the job requirements in terms of job description, job specifications, and so forth.

Al Smith should be given approximately five minutes to prepare notes on how he will handle the interview with Mary Jones. While the individual playing the role of Al Smith is preparing his approach for interviewing Mrs. Jones, the other members of the group should individually make notes and determine whether or not they would hire Mary Jones. Assuming they would at least give her a fair hearing for the job, they should list questions they would like to ask and what information they would like to obtain.

## EXHIBIT 2.1

**APPLICATION FOR EMPLOYMENT**
(Use Pencil or Typewriter)
NOTE: Applications will be kept active for one year

TEST CARD SENT _____

**Name** (As shown on Social Security Card)
(Print) (Last) JONES  (First) MARY  (Middle) A

**Social Security Number** 493-36-0036

Local Address J45 MAIN PLACE    Telephone 443-8113
Other Address _____    Telephone _____

Single ☐   Married ☒
Engaged ☐   Widow(er) ☐   Separated ☐   Divorced ☐

**Date of Birth** JULY 29, 1937
Number of Dependents _____   Ages of Children _____
**Height** 5'2"   **Weight** 105   Military Status _____

Physical Limitations? NO (Explain on back)   U.S. Citizen YES
Have you received injury compensation? NO
Have you been arrested for other than traffic violations? NO

Any medical or psychiatric treatment during the past five years? _____

Name of Wife or Husband HAROLD   His-Her Occupation STORE MANAGER   Where Employed WHITE'S DEPT. STORE

How long do you plan to work INDEF.   Date Available NOW   Hours I Can Work NORMAL BUSINESS

**TYPE OF WORK DESIRED**
1. SECRETARIAL   2. _____   3. _____
Full Time X   Part Time _____   Permanent Full Time _____   Temporary Part Time _____

**PREVIOUS EMPLOYMENT** (List most recent job first - include military service)

Name of Employer ADV. MGMT. CONSULTANTS
Street 3100 MADISON
City _____   Name of Supervisor MR. CARNES
Employed From JULY 1968   To DATE
Job Duties PERSONAL SECRETARY
Monthly Pay 550/MO.
Reason for Leaving FIRM GOING OUT OF BUSINESS

Name of Employer PARTIME TYPING AGENCY
Street 1301 WHITNEY
City _____   Name of Supervisor MR. EWALD
Employed From JAN 1964   To JULY 1968
Job Duties TYPING - PART TIME
Monthly Pay BY JOB
Reason for Leaving FULL-TIME

Name of Employer _____
Street _____
City _____   Name of Supervisor _____
Employed From _____   To _____
Job Duties _____
Monthly Pay _____
Reason for Leaving _____

(Additional employment may be listed on back)

Relatives Working   Name HAROLD (ABOVE) Relationship HUSBAND
Name _____ Relationship _____

**EDUCATION**
Circle highest year completed
Grade 1 2 3 4 5 6 7 8
High School 1 2 3 (4)
Business School 1 2
College or University 1 2 3 (4)
Undergraduate   Major FINE ARTS   Year Graduated 1959
Institution UNIV. OF KANSAS   Doc
Graduate Degree Mas   Doc
Major _____   Year Graduated _____
Institution _____

OTHER SCHOOLS OR SPECIAL TRAINING

**SKILLS** (Check)   DATE
Duplicating Machines _____
Adding Machine ✓
Calculator _____
Key Punch _____
Tabulating Mach. _____
Typewriter (Elect) ✓
Typewriter (Manual) ✓
Dictation Machine ✓
Shorthand — any system ✓

**TEST SCORES**
Do not write Below
Name _____
Number _____
Problems _____
Vocabulary _____
Filing _____
Spelling _____
Typing Speed 90/MIN
Typing Accuracy _____
Shorthand Speed 130/MIN
Shorthand Accuracy _____

**IMPORTANT**
I understand that giving false information is cause for discharge. A loyalty oath and a physical examination may be required.

Signature Mary A. Jones

## SPECIFIC INSTRUCTIONS TO BE GIVEN TO BOTH
## AL SMITH AND MARY JONES

Once all observers and the individual playing the role of Al Smith have determined what information they want to gather from Mary Jones, information not on the application form, the interview can be started. The interview should be handled in accordance with the normal rules of role-playing; each person should give honest answers reflecting how he would respond if he were actually involved in the situation. When the role-playing interview is concluded, Al Smith must announce to the members of the group whether or not he would hire Mary Jones. Then each member of the group must say what he would do on the basis of the information at hand.

## HOW TO CRITIQUE THE EMPLOYMENT INTERVIEW

A general discussion will follow the interview. Each member of the group will discuss why he decided to hire or not to hire Mrs. Jones. The individual who played Al Smith should, of course, explain his decision and the reasons he selected the approach he used in the interview.

After the reasons for wanting to hire or not to hire Mrs. Jones are all made clear, the group should evaluate how well the individual playing the role of Al Smith actually performed. Did he handle the personal relationship well and elicit all the necessary information? Was he more of a talker than a listener? Did he actually apply the rules for active listening? Did he use silence to his advantage? Was he adept at asking encouraging questions? Was he encouraging toward the person who played the role of Mary Jones? Did he use the technique of restating what Mary said to get additional information? Did he close the interview quickly and effectively?

Al Smith should also be critiqued on whether or not he retained good control over the interview situation. Were the questions he asked well designed to extract information tactfully, or did they simply require a Yes or No answer? Was his approach flexible? Did he extend normal social courtesies? Did he allow her sufficient time to respond with all the pertinent information she might offer? Did he make intelligent use of the material submitted by Mrs. Jones in her résumé? Did he guide the conversation back to essentials if it began to drift off the subject? Did he make tactful transitions if difficult or possibly embarrassing issues came up, ones not critical to the interview?

An Information-Gathering Interview
The Coffee Problem

**THE SITUATION** *(Read by or to all participants)*

This situation involves an information-gathering interview in which the boss must counsel with an employee. The problem arose because Susan Stone refused to make coffee for the office force. Furthermore, all the other girls, Mary, Alice, Jane, and Dorothy, have also refused to make coffee.

Bill Ward is Susan's boss and manager of the office. It is basically his problem, because in the last three years the girls have taken turns making coffee for the entire office, each girl taking one day a week. It has now been three days since the girls have made coffee. The fellows in the office are complaining and crabbing, morale is at a low ebb, and the situation, to say the least, is a mite ridiculous. However, all the girls are adamant in their refusal to make coffee and all the men are just as adamant in their feeling that coffee should be available and that they should not have to make it or wash up afterward. As a result, people have either been going without their coffee and complaining, or leaving the building and walking four blocks to the nearest coffee shop. This takes them out of the office for about thirty minutes, which Bill Ward considers too long. Furthermore, if coffee were brought back to the office from this distance, it would be cold.

In an effort to resolve the situation Bill thought that he would go to the initial source of the problem. So far as he could tell, it first started when Susan Stone one day simply decided that, even though it was her turn,

125

she was not going to make coffee. He has therefore called Susan into his office to determine what is wrong and what can be done to resolve the situation.

## REQUIREMENTS OF THE SITUATION

The role-playing situation involved here is that of a counseling interview. Three role players are needed: one person to play Susan Stone, one to play Don VanDyke, one to play Bill Ward; and one or more persons should serve as observers. The entire group can, of course, serve as observers, or one individual can be designated to observe the three named role-players. If the group is large enough, groups of four can be established and several people can play each of the roles.

## SPECIFIC INSTRUCTIONS FOR BILL WARD

The individual who is to play Bill Ward is to have read the general instructions above and must be given the following information:

Susan Stone is a young, attractive divorcée who is supporting her mother and an eight-year-old son. She must work for a living, and has been employed by Acme, Inc., under Bill Ward's supervision, for some three years.

Sue, as she is usually called, is generally friendly and light-hearted. However, she does occasionally fly off the handle and sometimes appears to be rather sensitive.

It has been brought to your attention that the reason that Susan refused to make coffee, and the reason the other girls followed suit, is that someone had made nasty comments about the taste of the coffee one day when Sue made it. You yourself know that all the girls use the same pot, the same coffee, the same measuring cup, and so forth. You have never noticed any difference in the taste of the coffee from day to day. You are concerned about the problem and wish to get to the bottom of it. Sue is now entering your office for a counseling interview.

When this counseling session is over, you can talk to Don VanDyke, if you so desire.

## SPECIFIC INSTRUCTIONS FOR SUSAN STONE

As Susan Stone you are a hard working, honest, serious employee of this organization. You have been here for a little more than three years. You are a divorcée and have to support not only your eight-year-old son but also your mother. You like your job, and you very definitely like the girls with whom you work. You get along extraordinarily well with them and you are pleased that they are supporting you in trying to win what you perceive is a tough battle at this point.

The trouble began when Don VanDyke and a couple of the other fellows in the office made some rather disparaging remarks about the quality of the coffee that you make. Actually, you had never objected to taking your turn at making the coffee for the office. You felt that it was one of those chores which had to be done. Furthermore, it was the kind of chore that girls were more or less expected to do, and you didn't mind doing your share. What's more, you had always been conscientious about how you made the coffee, following the generally established formula that the other girls use. You never felt that your coffee tasted any better or any worse than anyone elses'; you never expected any praise, but you certainly didn't expect any criticism. The other day Don VanDyke, out of eyesight and earshot of the others, but nevertheless in front of you, said that your coffee was the "foulest tasting stuff" that he had ever drunk. After making that statement, he stuck the cup under the water faucet, turning it on and letting the water and coffee run out slowly down the drain. He said, "This stuff is so strong that it will eat up the pipes if we don't cut it with water before we flush it." You were hurt and angry as a result of this gesture and, needless to say, greatly antagonistic toward Don VanDyke.

When you told the other girls what had happened between you and Don VanDyke, they suggested that you simply quit making coffee. At first you were against this because you really felt that it was your place as well as theirs to make the coffee. You appreciated very much the fact that the girls were willing to give you support, but you really didn't feel that you should punish the whole office just because Don VanDyke was such a jerk. Furthermore, you were aware of the fact that Don had never liked you very well since the time he backed into your car in the parking lot and had to pay for having it repaired. It cost him $117 because he hadn't wanted to file a claim against his insurance because of his bad driving record.

You hadn't really wished to make a fuss out of the coffee situation, but the other girls were adamant about it because they, too, disliked Don. As a result, they made a pact, agreeing that for at least a month none of the girls would make coffee. You have decided not to tell the boss (Bill Ward) about this pact because it would only embroil him in a situation in which you feel he needn't become involved. Bill is a very nice likeable guy. You really feel that he is the kind of guy that you can talk to, and you feel a great deal of allegiance toward him.

Bill has just now called for you to come to his office, and you are sure that it is something about the coffee situation. You don't know what you are going to tell him. In spite of your loyalty to Bill, you know that the girls would look down on you if you ratted on them.

## SPECIFIC INSTRUCTIONS FOR DON VANDYKE

You, Don VanDyke, consider yourself quite a swinger and ladies' man. You are not married, and certainly you are not interested in getting married, but you do like to chase the women. Ever since you came to work at this company, you have been trying to make an impression on Susan Stone, but she seems to be absolutely oblivious of the fact that you exist. One day, fooling around and trying to get her attention, you inadvertently backed into her car. You felt like a fool for having done it, and besides that, it cost you something like $117 to have her car repaired and another $75 for the damage that you did to your own car.

Not only did you feel that you made a fool of yourself in front of Susan, but she has been rather grouchy ever since as a result of the incident. You have pretty well chalked her off your list as one of the girls you would most like to date. If you are honest with yourself, you rather resent the fact that she is considered attractive and fun by the other men in the office.

The other day, just horsing around and not really knowing why you did it, you made a big scene in front of Susan about her coffee, pouring it down the drain, and commenting that the stuff was so strong that it had to be cut with water or it would eat up the pipes. Susan got very indignant about this, you recall, but you had thought nothing of it until the next day when there was no coffee. You are reasonably sure that the reason the coffee is not being made is because Susan ratted on you to the other girls. You feel that it was a rather trivial incident, and that it is quite childish of Susan and the other girls to behave as they are doing. More specifically, however, you are concerned that the word will get back to the boss (Bill Ward) that you are the cause of it all. You know that Bill likes to have his coffee ready in the morning, as do most of the other guys, and they are beginning to complain about not having any. The girls haven't really said why they refuse to make coffee; they simply refuse to make it. That is just like women. They are a bunch of dummies anyway, and they do crazy, kooky things. You hope that your boss doesn't find out about what is going on because he hasn't shown much sympathy toward your liberal points of view. Primarily, however, you would hate to lose your job because you would probably lose your car if you did.

Bill Ward however has just asked you to step into his office. You are worried that he may want to see you about the coffee incident because you saw Susan Stone go into his office a short while ago.

## HOW TO CRITIQUE THE CASE

The way the case of the counseling interview must be handled, in a word, is diplomatically. Obviously, in the critique session, Bill Ward should be judged as to whether or not he got the necessary information from Susan Stone and/or Don VanDyke as to what caused the problem. Ward would be rated high in a counseling session if he was able to discover information about a number of important points. Did he learn about the wreck? Did he discover that Sue Stone was not at all aware of the fact that Don VanDyke would have liked to date her but never really came out in the open about it? Did he learn the whole story about the coffee incident, about its being poured down the drain, and so forth? Was he able to persuade Sue to reveal why the other girls are united in their bond not to make coffee for a period of a month?

Before you give Bill Ward high marks, consider how he elicited this information. Would you say he made a deft use of questions and the use of silence? Did he direct the conversation skillfully? Was he encouraging? Or did he get the information by badgering Sue, by threatening perhaps to fire her, or by assuming an aggressive role? If so, he is to be given low marks even though he got the information. Such a performance would aggravate the situation, cause him to lose any rapport he had, and probably result in an uncomfortable atmosphere in the office. Probably no one would willingly and cheerfully make coffee in the future.

If Bill Ward elected to talk also with Don VanDyke, you must consider how well he handled this interview. Was he antagonistic toward him, and so forth? The critique would follow much the same course as the previous one.

*Special Note:* If Bill Ward did *not* talk to Don VanDyke, this case can be continued as a disciplinary interview in which Bill will be given the role of calling in Don VanDyke for a disciplinary/counseling session.

# Case 4　　Disciplinary Interview
The Water Boy

**THE SITUATION** *(Read to or by all participants)*

This case involves a disciplinary problem in which Frank Vetter, supervisor of the delivery and service section of Acme Water Distributors, must take some action. The situation is as follows.

Hank Vetter's primary responsibility is to train and motivate delivery salesmen to deliver distilled water in bottles to offices and homes and to sell or solicit new accounts. The organization sells bottled water, electric coolers, and cups to commercial and domestic accounts. Their salesmen carry the company's products into their areas and are the sole representatives of the company in their respective areas. Most of these delivery salesmen take over established routes, and they average about $800 a month in commissions. Quite often individuals who settle into this work are satisfied with that level of income and don't really wish to increase sales or their efforts in performing the job. The men who become complacent are not considered satisfactory performers, but they at least do the job and are looked upon as being all right.

The specific problem involved here, however, concerns John McMahon. Complaints have been received in the past that John was rude and arrogant toward customers, but the present situation is virtually unbelievable. A customer has complained that he used obscene language and caused what may have been malicious mischief. The matter has gone so far that a representative from the city manager's office, in a community in which John McMahon works, has just notified Hank Vetter that the city is considering revoking the company's solicitor's license for door-to-door selling

135

because of what John has done. What the complaint boils down to is that a Mrs. Barrows has accused John of using vile, vulgar language, of harrassment, and of personal insult. She has complained to the city fathers. Unfortunately, Mrs. Barrows is quite prominent in the community.

## REQUIREMENTS OF THE SITUATION

In this role-playing situation we need someone to play the role of Hank Vetter, someone to be John McMahon, and at least one observer. As in many of the other cases in this book, the instructor using these cases may choose to divide a large group into groups of three in which each person can play one of the principals—Vetter, McMahon, or observer.

## SPECIFIC INSTRUCTIONS FOR HANK VETTER

You, Hank Vetter, are a supervisor for the Acme Water Distributors. One of your employees, John McMahon, who delivers your products and solicits from door-to-door for both residential and commercial accounts in the southwest section of Jefferson City, has recently become the subject of numerous complaints. John has worked for you for a year and a half, and you haven't thought too much about the complaints about him in the past. Initially they seemed to be minor grievances, such as parking his truck in driveways or in other areas where he shouldn't. But lately you have begun to receive complaints that he is rude and arrogant toward the customers.

The crowning incident concerning John McMahon just occurred today. A representative from the city manager's office has notified you that the city may revoke your license for door-to-door solicitation for your water coolers. You are greatly upset, although after talking with this representative you are reasonably confident that the city will not actually lift the licence.

This particular incident concerning John McMahon evidently unfolded as follows. After parking his truck (at least this time legally), John began to engage in his house-to-house solicitation of people who might be customers for bottled water. On his particular route the regular and prospective customers are usually older people who need distilled water for health reasons. You have known for some time that John evidently doesn't like to call on older customers; he himself is young, in his early 20's. The incident was reported in this way: John went to the door of a Mrs. Barrows' home and rang the doorbell. Mrs. Barrows came to the door, immediately ascertained that it was a salesman, and slammed the door in John's face. John at this point reportedly made an obscene gesture through the glass toward the woman, and turned to walk away. The woman watched him for a while, ostensibly to be sure that he was leaving, and found out that in fact he did not leave, but followed the sidewalk around to the back of the house.

He went to the back door and knocked. She went to the door to tell him to leave. She opened the door, but before she could tell him to leave, John yelled the following at her and turned around and ran: "I hope you are not as mean and crazy as that old bitch that lives around front." As John ran from the house evidently he again made what the lady considered obscene gestures; then he hopped in his truck and drove away.

You feel that, beyond question, John did essentially what the woman reported to the representative from the city manager's office. His behavior may possibly not have been as bad as was stated. You are not sure whether or not you should fire John; in fact, you think you shouldn't. However, some disciplinary action must be taken. You are now going to counsel with John to determine the exact facts of the situation and then decide how you will handle the disciplinary matter.

## SPECIFIC INSTRUCTIONS FOR JOHN MCMAHON

You, John McMahon, age 23, have worked for Acme Water Distributors for a year and a half. You are a delivery salesman for bottled water and electric water coolers. You prefer servicing commercial accounts because working people are always nicer and friendlier. Then, too, it is easy to find a place to park because you can park in delivery zones. Besides, it is usually warm in the winter and cool in the summer in the offices that you deliver the water to, and you occasionally get to meet a few gals as a result of having to contact the receptionist or secretary to set things up for the delivery.

One thing that you don't like about your job is having to make calls on people in residential areas. It is not so bad if you are just delivering refills to regular customers, but you really hate to contact new customers. You know you really don't like selling, particularly to fussy old people with health problems.

You got into a bit of a pickle the other day on this door-to-door bit. You are afraid now that you are really in for it because you have heard that someone from the city manager's office has been in touch with your boss, Hank Vetter. You figure it must be about what you did over at that old lady's place the other day.

What happened over there ran as follows: You parked your truck and walked up to the door to give her the pitch. However, the minute she opened the door and realized you wanted to sell something, she screamed "Get out of here!" and slammed the door in your face. She did it with such violence that you almost fell off her porch. The porch was only a tiny stoop anyway, and she keeps it cluttered with big potted plants. You were kind of waving your arms in an attempt to catch your balance while she stood there watching you through the door. As you started to walk away you figured that this was the last time that you would try to sell anything to old lady Barrows, no matter what the boss said.

At this point however, a strange thought occurred to you. Your brother, who used to sell vacuum cleaners door-to-door, had told you of a trick that he used to play on people to kind of lift his spirits when they acted like Mrs. Barrows had just done. What he did was to go around to the back door and knock on it. When the person who had slammed the front door came to the back door, he's say something to them like "Gee, I hope you're not as grouchy as the person who lives around front." And then he'd run off. So you thought you'd try it because you were especially down in the dumps. So you did. After Mrs. Barrows came to the door you said something to the effect of "Gee, I hope you're not as grumpy as that old bat that lives around front," and started to run off. You hadn't really been watching where you were going, and you nearly fell over a lawn chair which was close to the walk. You almost had to jump over the chair and when you landed you twisted your ankle, so you stopped running. When you reached down to rub your ankle, you remember hearing Mrs. Barrows screaming "I'll get you for this, young man," and you were really frightened.

Well, it now looks like the old battle-axe meant what she said. The boss has just called you in, and you have a feeling that this is what he is going to talk to you about.

## HOW TO CRITIQUE THE COUNSELING INTERVIEW

The critique of the counseling interview at this point largely depends upon how the person who plays Hank Vetter handles himself. First off, he should engage in information-gathering techniques to determine what, in fact, was the substance of the case. Obviously, the individual playing the role of Hank Vetter has had the story told him by the city manager's representative. However, he does not have the story of John McMahon. If he handles the situation correctly, Vetter will get McMahon's story by asking questions, directing McMahon's train of thought, making transitions, drawing him out, and then confronting McMahon with any variations in the story which develop. The individual who plays the role of Hank Vetter may, of course, carry the interview on to the point of meting out some kind of punishment to John McMahon—perhaps a formal reprimand, possibly a day or so off without pay. If this is done, it should be done forthrightly and tactfully, consistent with whatever the interviewer thinks is an appropriate punishment under the situation. However, it must be clear that, if the individual who plays Hank Vetter does elect to penalize McMahon, he has engaged in the practice of corrective discipline, rather than punitive discipline. That is, he should have done something which was designed to salvage John McMahon as a salesman, unless, of course, he decided to fire McMahon. Finally, if Vetter does elect to fire John, he should be doing so on the basis of having full and sufficient cause—in this case something to substantiate the fact that John did indulge in obscenities or obscene gestures in the situation. Any punishment should be fitting in terms of what he could establish as true after his conversation with McMahon. The observer should be able to judge whether Vetter's actions are fair and realistic.

Exit Interview
The Case of Bob Gray

---

**THE SITUATION** *(Read to or by all participants)*

This case concerns an exit interview with Bob Gray who has just turned in his resignation, to take effect at the end of the week. The personnel manager from the main office has come over to interview the man and find out, if possible, the real reason for his quitting. He has been doing a good job as head of the sales force.

**REQUIREMENTS OF THE SITUATION**

This situation involves two role-players, öne to be Bob Gray and one to be the personnel manager from the home office, plus any number of observers. When the person who is to be Bob Gray has familiarized himself with the facts, he is then in a position to be interviewed by the personnel manager, a person who is practicing his skills at exit interviewing. The other members of the group should watch and be prepared to critique the way the interview is handled.

## SPECIFIC INSTRUCTIONS FOR THE INTERVIEWER
(The personnel manager from the home office)

The person who is to play the role of the personnel manager from the main office and do the interviewing must *not* read over the case material. He should go into the case cold, as he would have to do in real life. All he needs to know is that Phil Katona is the branch manager of the Muskegan office, Ray Engel is in charge of the sales section of the office, and Bob Gray has just resigned as head of the claims section of the office.

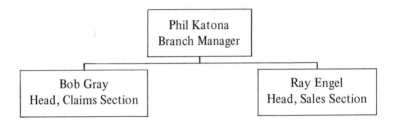

**SPECIFIC INSTRUCTIONS FOR BOB GRAY** (to be given *only* to the individual who is to play the role and to the observers)

The events as they happened can be described as follows: Phil Katona is the branch manager in charge of the Muskegan office of the Michigan Insurance Corporation. He had just arrived at work and was grabbing a cup of coffee when Ray Engel approached him. Ray is head of the sales department of this branch office. He is a happy kind of guy and easy enough for Phil to supervise, but he was always bringing minor problems to Phil. This morning it was just some more of the same. Ray happened to have a problem with one of his clerk typists. She was upset and hurt because she had overheard a couple of the salesmen telling some off-color stories, and Ray didn't know what he should do about it. So he brought the problem to Phil who hadn't even had time to get to work on the report that he had to send in to the main office that day.

Even though Phil knew that his other work was pressing, he decided to listen to Ray's problem, so he said, "Okay, Ray, what's the trouble?" Ray immediately tried to tell him everything at once. From what Phil could gather, Donna had come to work at eight o'clock, and was sitting at her desk when Charles Williams and Bill Burkheart, two of the old-time salesmen, had come in. Charles had been telling Bill about his bowling scores the night before when he got off on some of the stories which he had heard at the lanes. Just as he got to the punch line, they were passing Donna's desk. Donna got all upset when she heard that dirtiest of words, and had come running into Ray's office, sobbing that she simply couldn't work in such vulgar surroundings and would Ray please speak to Charles and Bill about it.

Just as Ray finished telling Phil about the incident, Bob Gray came charging into Phil's office obviously madder than blazes. Bob was the claims supervisor and was a nice enough guy, only he had a tendency to be both outspoken and impudent at times. Without even excusing himself, Bob started raising cain about Gary Jones. Gary had just transferred to Bob's section from Ray's section (sales). Although Gary had had a good deal of experience in handling claims, he had had no experience in interviewing people. Bob was angry now because Gary had accepted a claimant's statement several days ago and had issued a check to the claimant. Bob felt that the payment was not justified.

It took both Phil and Ray a full two minutes to get Bob calmed down enough to get the story straight. But as soon as Bob was able to gain his composure he started out again—but this time he was on Ray. Bob started yelling that it was Ray's fault Gary was such a lousy employee, and that if he (Bob) had been responsible for training him he would have seen to it that the guy had learned more than just how to sell insurance policies.

Ray got mad when Bob made disparaging remarks about Ray's competence as a trainer. He made it very clear that since he was in charge of the sales section, he would naturally train his people to be salesmen, *not* claims reviewers. Then he told Bob, "If you were such a damn good trainer, you would train your new claims people in how to process claims properly anyway. It's not my fault that you want everybody to do your job for you."

At this point Bob really popped his cork and told Phil that he was quitting as of the end of the week. This is the situation as the Manager of Personnel of the parent company begins his interview with Bob to determine why he gave his notice to quit.

### Additional Information for the Person Playing the Role of Bob Gray
(*not* to be given to the individual playing the role of exit interviewer)

1. Bob and Ray had never really gotten along well together in their previous working relationships.

2. Bob feels that Phil is a wishy-washy supervisor.

3. Bob feels that Ray is Phil's "pet" and that his own chances of going anywhere in the organization are blocked.

4. Bob's wife doesn't like his working in Muskegan. He had been transferred from Detroit, the location of his wife's former home and where she wants to live.

5. Bob really feels that most of the employees in the organization are poorly trained.

6. Bob also feels that most employees are not highly motivated because of the low pay scale in the company.

## HOW TO CRITIQUE THE INTERVIEW

The way to test whether or not the interviewer has done a good job is to compare the information which he gets—about what happened and why Bob is leaving the organization—with the real facts of the situation. If the interviewer not only brings out all the facts accurately, but also, as a result of the role-playing situation, comes up with accurate ideas as to any personality conflicts between Bob Gray, Phil Katona, and Ray Engels, he should get a good score. Bonus points should be given if he was also able to detect Bob's underlying resentment toward the company and the fact that he might have personal reasons for wanting to make a change.

# Case 6     Structured Interview
Induction of Employee

---

## THE SITUATION *(Read by or to all participants)*

The following case contains nothing more than a detailed list of information which the interviewer must communicate to a "hire." The purpose behind this case is to acquaint supervisors with the problems inherent in the relatively simple situation of telling new employees certain facts about the organization which they are joining.

Having a "grocery list" of items to tell the new person serves as a reminder and assures thoroughness. The individual playing the role of the interviewer can use the list as a guide. It will be noted, as the case is played, that those who are not really adept at using a structured interview form frequently fall into the trap of reading the list to the interviewee, not bothering to explain the implication of various points and seldom, if ever, giving the new hire an opportunity to ask questions.

## REQUIREMENTS OF THE SITUATION

This case requires two role players—one to play the role of the boss, Sam Jones, who is to conduct the induction interview with a new hire, Bill Barker. The other person is to assume the role of the new employee, Bill Barker. All others in the group may serve as observers of the interview.

## SPECIFIC INSTRUCTIONS FOR SAM JONES, The Manager

You, Sam Jones, have just hired Bill Barker. The following is a list of the information you are to discuss with him. If you need specific facts, you are to assume that the company's policy for the role is the same as the policy of the company for which you work in real life.

### Checklist of Subjects to Be Covered during an Induction Interview for Any New Hire of the Company

1. Tell him something about the history of the company—the founder, president, and so forth.

2. Explain what the company's products or services are and the major operations involved in making those products or providing those services.

3. Explain precisely how his services will fit into making the product or providing the service. (It is a good idea to assume he will be taking a specific job with which you are familiar.)

4. If training is necessary, tell him who will be responsible for him.

5. Explain what happens if any difficulties should occur between him and his immediate superior.

6. Cover organizational rules and regulations concerning

   a)   the wages he will receive,

   b)   when he will be paid and how much will be withheld,

   c)   when he is to report for duty and when he is to leave,

   d)   the arrangements for lunch periods and coffee breaks,

   e)   the possibility for overtime work and overtime pay provisions,

   f)   what happens in respect to safety and accident problems,

   g)   the company's holiday and vacation policy,

   h)   what happens if a person is late to work,

   i)   the company's policy about sick leave,

   j)   what happens if he has to miss a day of work, excused or otherwise, and how it affects his pay,

k)   what happens if he has a grievance—how to file it, etc.,

l)   how he is supposed to dress,

m)  where he is to park his car, keep his personal belongings, etc.,

n)   what he is to do about company identification,

o)   what organizational rules are in respect to security.

7. Explain fringe benefits such as accident and sickness insurance, hospital insurance, life insurance, pensions, employee discounts, use of company recreational facilities, and so forth.

8. Cover in detail with him the opportunities that he may have for promotion in the organization, or at least what his future holds for him.

## SPECIFIC INSTRUCTIONS FOR BILL BARKER

You are to assume you are just being hired by Sam Jones. He is now conducting an induction interview. You may ask any questions you wish.

## HOW TO CRITIQUE THE INDUCTION INTERVIEW

The interviewer should be given a good score on conducting the interview if he conveys to the new hire, with ease and grace, all the information on the detailed list of subjects. Was he aware of the reactions of the other person? Did he explain any information that didn't seem to be clear? Would the new employee go away with a good feeling toward the company as a result of the interview?

## Performance Appraisal
Carver and Company, Incorporated*

**THE SITUATION** *(Read by or to all participants)*

The following case is designed to be representative of a performance-appraisal situation. The situation concerns Sam Carver's problem in having to tell his brother George that he is really not up to the task of taking over the organization for Sam, even though Sam is having to quit because of his loss of vision.

The time has come for Sam Carver to face a serious situation. During the past two years he has been losing the vision in his right eye, and now the doctor has confirmed that his left eye will also follow the same process. He has a lot to think about.

Sam's father started Carver and Company about fifty years ago. For many years he operated a lumber yard in one small midwest city, and then he opened yards in three small nearby communities. Later he added a line of building supplies, and still later he branched out into sales of fixtures, appliances, and related home building needs.

When Sam took over the business at his father's retirement he expanded the retail sales operation, and later he established lumber yards in two other small communities. He also greatly expanded the firm's construction activities, at first in home improvements, and later in construction jobs. The firm's largest project was the construction of a school building.

---

*Written by Edward J. Morrison, Professor of Management, University of Colorado.

The firm had also purchased land for speculative development, and they had built custom homes and some houses for speculative sales.

As he looked at the organization and operation of the firm Sam was not sure that things were in the best of shape. An organization chart is shown in Chart 7-1. Sam's brother George worked for the firm, but George was not the businessman that Sam was. As Sam saw it, "George couldn't smell a profitable deal if it were on his upper lip." Sam was reluctant to let George take over the firm. Sam would like to have his son take over the business, but he sadly acknowledged that his son who was a music major at the state university had shown no interest in the family business. And Sam really burned when he thought of relinquishing control to someone not "in the family."

There was only one man in the organization in whom Sam had very much confidence. That was Charlie Huggins. Huggins had a liberal arts degree from a small college in the state, and after coming with Carver he had studied accounting by correspondence courses. He had reorganized the firm's bookkeeping system and arranged an up-to-date financial system. In general, he was very competent. Sam had taken the speculative housing and land development project away from George when George seemed to falter, and he had given it to Charlie, who really made it go. It was one of the firm's more profitable ventures.

The other members of "top management" at Carver included Bill Conover, Tom Weeks, and Dave Thompson. Conover was 65, did the purchasing for the company, and had held that job under Sam's father, even before Sam joined the firm. Tom Weeks was 55, ran the retail store, and in part looked over the operations of the lumber yards. Dave Thompson, 50, was boss of building projects under construction, although Sam himself was the top man in this area and in fact ran the department. As Sam thought about it, none of these fellows really made big decisions—he had always done that. In fact, only Charlie Huggins ever carried much weight in their top management meetings. Sam also was not impressed particularly with any of the younger men in the organization. Although several were good workers and loyal employees, he didn't see any managers among them, with a couple of possible exceptions.

## REQUIREMENTS OF THE SITUATION

This role-playing case requires two players: one for the role of Sam Carver, President of Carver and Company, Inc., and one for the role of George Carver, Sam's brother and Manager of Retail and Wholesale Sales.

**CHART 7-1.**

CARVER AND COMPANY, INC.
ORGANIZATION CHART

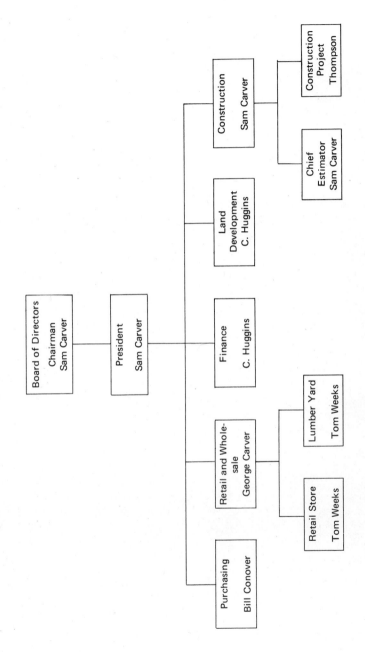

## SPECIFIC INSTRUCTIONS FOR SAM CARVER, PRESIDENT OF THE COMPANY

You are Sam Carver, and you are ready to step out as president of Carver and Company, Inc. You do not intend to make George your successor as president of Carver and Company, Inc. You are now preparing to talk to your brother George, to conduct what is, in effect, a performance-appraisal interview. You will review the following notes, and then ask him to join you.

### Notes about George

1. He creates a morale problem in the organization.

2. He's tactless in dealing with customers.

3. He's naive and can be duped into making unwise decisions.

4. He isn't especially bright.

5. He is extremely good with paper and pencil and can figure deals well.

6. He has a reputation among his fellow workers of being a "Don't blame it on me" type.

7. He's extremely good at grinding out the work and getting the job done.

8. He's a clock watcher and always takes his compensatory time.

9. He's responsible for at least one man's quitting in exasperation.

10. One of his salesmen is apparently planning to quit.

11. He's extremely religious, does not drink, and looks down his nose at those who do.

12. He's an extremely sensitive man and has been known to break down and cry.

13. He has a problem about truthfulness—he doesn't always tell the truth, yet he would deny that he ever told a lie of any proportions.

14. He deludes himself into thinking that he has a tremendous rapport with people.

15. He doesn't think that Sam appreciates what he does.

## SPECIFIC INSTRUCTIONS FOR GEORGE CARVER, BROTHER OF THE PRESIDENT OF THE COMPANY

You are George Carver, brother to Sam Carver, who is president of Carver and Company, Inc. Your father started the company about fifty years ago. Sam took over the management of the business from your father. At one time you and Sam had equal shares of the business, but because you got involved in some poor dealings in investment property, you had to sell your share of the business to Sam. This didn't especially bother you from the standpoint of running the company because you had never been especially excited about the business anyway. However, the firm has prospered, and you would like to have a more substantial cut in the profits of the organization.

You know that Sam is having difficulty with his eyes. For the past two years he has been losing the vision in his right eye, and he was just informed by his doctor that his left eye would also gradually go in the same way. You know that Sam is thinking about stepping down, and you think that you may have a chance to succeed him as president of the company. You would like to do this, and feel that you are qualified. Furthermore, you are convinced that the business ought to stay in the family.

Sam has called you and wants to discuss with you the future direction of Carver and Company. You are going in to see Sam now.

## HOW TO CRITIQUE THE APPRAISAL INTERVIEW

The person playing Sam Carver should be critiqued in respect to the way he handled George. Was he successful in making George realize

1. How he stands in the organization generally?

2. That he is not in line to succeed Sam as president?

3. What his personal strengths and weaknesses are?

If Sam puts George down too strenuously or lets the situation get out of control and emotions run high, he should get low marks. And if he strings George along and doesn't make the facts clear, he should get low marks.

# Case 8

## Combined Coaching, Performance-Appraisal, and Review Interview
### The Case of Bill Kerns

---

## THE SITUATION *(Read to or by all participants)*

The following case is a combined coaching, performance-appraisal, and review situation. In the role-playing situation Norm Douglas is to review Bill Kern's progress as a salesman in the organization. The chief problem which must be discussed is Bill's carelessness about coming to work regularly and on time. Another subject must be faced: Bill's style of living is having an adverse effect on his performance at work. Furthermore, he seems to take too many liberties with his expense statements. We need to have a role player assume the position of Norm Douglas who is the sales manager and another man to take the role of Bill Kerns, the salesman. Any number of observers can be used.

## REQUIREMENTS OF THE SITUATION

The person who is to be Norm Douglas is to read the instructions for the sales manager. He must prepare himself to review Bill's performance with him and let him know what things need improving. Furthermore, because this is a performance appraisal *and* coaching situation, the individual who plays the role of Norm Douglas must plan to discuss what corrective action will be necessary to bring Bill's performance up to a satisfactory level.

## SPECIFIC INSTRUCTIONS FOR NORM DOUGLAS, SALES MANAGER

You are Norm Douglas, the sales manager for Plantey Distributors. Bill Kerns, one of your salesmen, has the job of calling on the smaller customers in your territory. You are not exactly pleased with some of the things that Bill is doing. Your assessment of his performance runs about as follows: Bill is a good word merchant and can talk himself out of almost any situation. He is virtually the stereotype of the salesman, and he comes on strong in that capacity. In his personal life Bill is a failure. He has been in business for himself, but he lost that business and had to file for bankruptcy. Bill could easily be a real con artist, if given the opportunity, and you have always questioned his honesty to some degree. Bill is currently separated from his wife and is about to be divorced. He suffers from a tremendous ego and has a great deal of drive and ambition. He gets carried away by his own enthusiasms and practically always ends up getting in over his head, especially financially. Bill's estranged wife is an outspoken individual who has always tried to cut Bill down in public. It seemed as though she was doing this in an effort to get him to get his feet on the ground. Obviously, it hasn't worked out very well.

Bill's personal life seems to be in a continual upheaval. Financially he is always playing a fine game of brinkmanship. Bill maneuvers very quickly, and is always having to cover checks at the bank and do other things of that nature. Bill talks an extremely good game and is, in fact, a pro when it comes to selling. Bill is not exactly a man's man, and he doesn't relate well on a personal basis with some of his fellow salesmen. However, this feature doesn't seem to detract from his ability to sell to customers. Bill is very loose with his charge cards. Several times Bill has been caught charging personal items on company cards. He has always covered by saying that he "just forgot to mention it and had intended to pay the company back" (and he always has *after* he's been confronted with the problem). Unfortunately, this practice is beginning to become chronic. Bill practically always takes liberties with his expense accounts—they are obviously padded and charges are frequently unsupported.

Bill seems to have an uncanny ability to size up prospects, and he seems to have a sixth sense which tells him when someone is, in fact, going to buy our product. However, in other areas he isn't very perceptive about people, and their reactions to him. In fact, it is doubtful that Bill will understand the purpose of this interview unless you, as Norm, clearly spell out these details to him.

## SPECIFIC INSTRUCTIONS FOR BILL KERNS, SALESMAN

You are Bill Kerns, age 28, a salesman for Plantey Distributors. Your boss, Norm Douglas, has just called you in for the annual performance appraisal and review. Practically always these are pointless interviews in which Norm takes the opportunity to kind of sound off about things which he doesn't like. For one thing, Norm is a pinch-penny, and he is always complaining to you about your expense accounts. You don't really fudge on your expense accounts, although you've got to admit that on occasion you have had to fake things to make up for expenses which you forgot to write down on other expense statements.

You've been having trouble at home with your wife and currently you aren't getting along very well with her. Since you walked out on her and took up bachelor quarters, you've been in quite a serious financial bind. You have extended your credit virtually to its limits, and you don't really know what to do about it. Over the past couple of months, on occasion, you have had to use your company charge cards (which you have in your possession) to charge items which you needed for your personal use. You have always repaid the company for these items, but you have been so strapped for cash recently that you haven't been in a hurry to get them repaid. Unfortunately, Norm has caught you a time or two on these items and has really gotten up tight about them.

You are afraid that this interview situation will be just some more of the same, with Norm really reading the riot act about your expense account. You don't know quite what you are going to do about it other than just try to talk your way through it. At least that is one thing that you have on your side: Norm is kind of a dullard and is reasonably gullible if you move quickly. You are trying to make your plans as to what you are going to say if he makes any accusations about your personal way of living, your family life, and especially your personal finances.

## HOW TO CRITIQUE THE INTERVIEW

Since the Bill Kerns case is a combined performance appraisal and coaching type of interview situation, what you should be looking for here is to see whether Norm Douglas was able to (1) get his message across to Bill, (2) get Bill to accept the fact that the message is correct, and (3) close the interview situation in such a way that it is reasonably likely that Bill is going to improve his performance and behavior as they concern the organization.

One strong point which must be made clear by Norm in this interview situation is that Bill must in fact correct abusing his expense account. The person playing the role of Norm Douglas will have done a good job if he keeps the thing on a positive plane, doesn't engage in arguments with Bill, yet manages to make Bill realize the importance of the criticisms. If Norm antagonized Bill, the situation did not come off well at all. Furthermore, if they debated several points or argued heatedly about them, it would detract from the effectiveness of the interview.

In summary, then, what Norm should have done was (1) face the facts squarely with Bill, (2) act very firm in his approach, (3) cover all those areas which are important to the problems of Bill's performance, (4) keep the situation above a personal plane, (5) stick to the facts of the situation, (6) avoid engaging in any cross-examination, (7) give Bill the opportunity to ask questions and to have points clarified, (8) clearly point out to Bill what he expects by way of improvement, (9) avoid trying to be funny or humorous, (10) keep from repeating himself after he has made his point, (11) keep in mind Bill's feelings, (12) get Bill to formulate his own action plan for changed behavior, and (13) try to tie together, at the close of the interview, the whole matter and indicate what results are expected.

Certainly Norm should *not* have (1) made promises to Bill which can't be kept, (2) given any unwarranted assurances to Bill or soft-pedalled any of the issues, (3) been impersonal or unfeeling in his approach, (4) tried to advise Bill about his personal life except as it directly concerned his work performance, (5) harped on several points, or (6) appeared as though he thought he knew it all about everything.

Norm should get an especially good mark on his information-imparting interview if he was successful in getting Bill to genuinely recognize what his problems are and if he managed the discussion in a firm but friendly way.

# INDEX

# Index